WORLD OF FOOTBALL

HOW TO PLAY LIKE A PRO

BLINK

bringing you closer

Published by Blink Publishing
3.25, The Plaza,
535 Kings Road,
Chelsea Harbour,
London, SW10 0SZ

www.blinkpublishing.co.uk

facebook.com/blinkpublishing
twitter.com/blinkpublishing

PB – 978-1-911274-44-5
Ebook – 978-1-911274-45-2
Special edition – 978-1-91127-476-6

All rights reserved. No part of the publication may be reproduced, stored in a retrieval system, transmitted or circulated in any form or by any means, electronic, mechanical, photocopying, recording or otherwise, without prior permission in writing of the publisher.

A CIP catalogue of this book is available from the British Library.

Cover design by Nathan Balsom
Design by Leard.co.uk

Printed and bound in Italy

1 3 5 7 9 10 8 6 4 2

Underlying copyright in the work © The F2 Freestylers
Text copyright © Blink Publishing Limited, 2016

Papers used by Blink Publishing are natural, recyclable products made from wood grown in sustainable forests. The manufacturing processes conform to the environmental regulations of the country of origin.

Every reasonable effort has been made to trace copyright holders of material reproduced in this book, but if any have been inadvertently overlooked the publishers would be glad to hear from them.

Blink Publishing is an imprint of the Bonnier Publishing Group
www.bonnierpublishing.co.uk

We dedicate this book to our incredible family and friends who have been there from the very beginning — The Original F2 Family.

Love, peace and tekkers x

THE F2 APP

GET THE ULTIMATE FOOTBALL SKILLS GUIDE FREE ON YOUR SCREEN!

Turbocharge your tekkers with The F2 App! Let Billy and Jez share their incredible showcase of skills and learn how to do it yourself with this exclusive digital content. From never-before-seen video tutorials, and helpful tips, to special features that bring your own football boot designs to life, The F2 will teach you how to play like a pro. And once you've honed your touch, you can upload your own skill videos and share them with The F2.

To access all the exclusive content, download the free app from the iTunes App Store or Google Play Store, launch the app and point your device's camera at the pages with the special phone icon (right). Here all of The F2's tips and special features will come to life on your screen!

*The F2 App by The F2 requires an Internet connection to be downloaded and can be used on iPhone, iPad or Android devices. For direct links to download the app and further information, visit www.blinkpublishing.co.uk.

Scan this page now for your first video!

CONTENTS

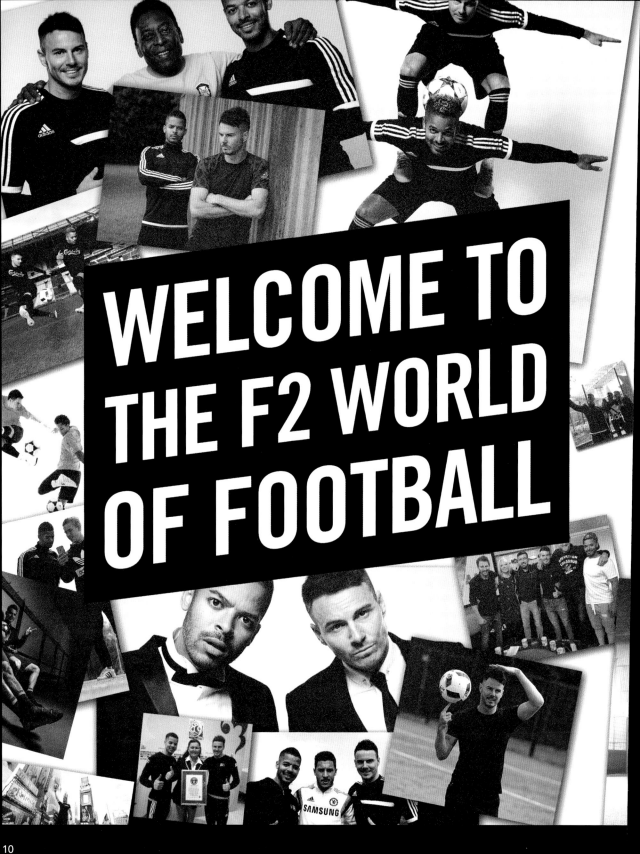

WELCOME TO THE F2 WORLD OF FOOTBALL

Yes guys!

We are about to share with you our story of how we became football superstars.

We'll take you right back to our childhoods, as we fell in love with the beautiful game. Then we'll show you how we arrived at two Premier League giants, the heartbreak along the way, and how we turned those setbacks into the biggest positive imaginable, by launching The F2 and conquering the planet.

We'll smuggle you behind the scenes of our amazing lives and share with you some cool untold stories of working with some of the game's very biggest names like Lionel Messi, Mesut Özil, Neymar and Pelé.

And that's just the start of the book! We'll also give you a step-by-step guide to becoming a football superstar, showing you how to perform the flicks and tricks, and how to carry yourself like a true legend.

Want to pull off moves like Neymar? Or to smash free kicks like Ronaldo? Or dribble like Lionel Messi? We show you how, with simple to follow guides.

We've even added an amazing complimentary app for you to download that will make the pages of this book come to life with exclusive videos, tricks and games.

So, what are you waiting for? Turn the page, read our stories, learn our tips and get out on that pitch and practise. There's no turning back now, we're gonna show you how to do it.

Love, peace and tekkers,
The F2.

THE F2 STORY:

ORIGINS: BILLY

Billy: To climb up onto my school roof was a massive task. It was a three-storey building. So I'd scramble up one storey and slide myself up a drainpipe to get onto the second storey. Then I'd clamber on top of the school sports hall. Finally, I'd arrived at my destination.

What was I doing up there? I was looking for lost footballs. That was where balls ended up after kids skied their shots or had a bit of a mare with a long pass or goal kick. My family didn't have a whole lot of money to chuck around when I was a kid, so the easiest way for me to get a new ball was to climb up to the top of the school and claim the lost ones.

I felt like Spider-Man. I was the only kid who climbed up there. I lived for football and the prize was well worth risking a fall. I've never not been interested in football.

Take a look through any of our family's photo albums and you'll see pictures of me at home, at school, on the street. There are pictures of me on holiday, some of them in England, some overseas. I'm all different ages in the photos. I'm sporting different haircuts (some of them absolute shockers) and different clothes in different eras. But in pretty much every single one I've got a football at my feet.

I played football 24/7, I played it everywhere, school, park, the AstroTurf, on the streets, even in my house – I couldn't stop kicking it around. It would drive my my older sister Jodie mad, she would get so angry with me playing indoors, because I'd knock things over.

She used to give me three warnings to stop playing, but of course this never stopped me. After the third warning she would open the back door and boot the ball about eight gardens down. One time she was so annoyed she went to the extreme of physically slashing a knife through my football in the hope I would finally stop. But she didn't know about my cheeky Spider-Man ploy at school, so I'd soon have a new one. She must have wondered where I got them from!

We both still laugh about it to this day. She says, 'It's ironic. How was I to know you'd go on to make a career out of juggling a football? And there was me trying to stop you doing it!' We have a good chuckle about it.

'I PLAYED FOOTBALL 24/7, I PLAYED IT EVERYWHERE, SCHOOL, PARK, THE ASTROTURF, ON THE STREETS, EVEN IN MY HOUSE I COULDN'T STOP KICKING IT AROUND.'

Throughout my childhood in Enfield in north London, my existence was dictated by football: watching football, playing football, and thinking about football. That was my day-to-day life, people. I really struggled academically at times, I must admit. I suffer from slight dyslexia, so in primary school I had my own teacher and in senior school I was in the lower sets.

But with football, I felt good. Even as a kid I knew that the game would be my life. Every morning when I went to school I'd kick the ball all the way. At break and lunchtime I ate hardly any food because I was too busy playing football. Come the evening, I'd be out playing until my mum called me in for dinner.

I couldn't get enough of it. My best mate Rooney (John Rooney, not Wayne!) would play football with me every day, but after a while he would go home to play computer games or watch TV, however I'd stay out there practising. I'd see that as time to practise skills on my own. I enjoyed any sort of kickabout, really, even on my tod.

I was a latecomer to playing with an actual team, though. I joined up for the first time when I was 11; most kids are already part of

'MY EXISTENCE WAS DICTATED BY FOOTBALL: WATCHING FOOTBALL, PLAYING FOOTBALL AND THINKING ABOUT FOOTBALL.'

the team by the time they're about eight. But when I'd been at primary school I'd not really wanted to get into a team.

I remember playing for my school: Lee Valley high school. We were the poorest school around. We had little in the way of funding and the behaviour of the kids could be terrible, to be honest. But we were good at sports, even though only one of the goals on the pitch had a net. Each team would kick into the net in one half and then into the empty goal in the second half. The amount of times I'd score a screamer of a goal into that empty net and the opposition would shout: 'It went over, it went over!' We'd end up having a massive argument and the teacher would have to decide whether to give the goal or not. It was so funny!

Near to my home there was an AstroTurf pitch. This was the hallowed ground to us as kids, the promised land! Officially, we weren't allowed there but, in case you haven't noticed yet, I don't let little obstacles like that get in my way for long. We used to climb in and each time the caretaker would eventually appear and chuck us out. He ended up threatening to get me expelled from school. He used to bolt the gate, but I managed to find a way to get it open. It's all naughty, I suppose, but that's how desperate I was to play football. And, of course, when I lost a ball or it went flat, it would be time for me to do the whole Spider-Man thing again.

I'd hide a scaffold board in the bushes, retrieve it when needed to put it at an angle against the school wall and climb up. Then there was plastic barbed wire blocking my way. But I'd thought of that and would be wearing a big puffa jacket so I could safely roll over it. Now I would be on the roof. I'd do a big run-up and leap so I could grab the box guttering and pull myself up onto the next ledge. I was on the top tier of the building.

If anyone kicked a ball onto the roof I'd get up there and claim it for myself. The caretaker never went up there – too lazy, probably.

I learned my climbing ability from my dad. He was and still is a roofer, so when I had the odd day off school he'd sometimes take me up with him. 'Don't tell your mum,' he'd say. To me he was a champion: he was climbing up five-storey buildings and tall, tall churches. I saw him as a superhero. So brave; maybe he was Spider-Man, and I was Spider-Kid!

He was really important to my progression in football, too. I loved looking to my dad when I was playing in games as a kid. Nothing beat the feeling of scoring a goal, looking over to him and seeing him jumping up and down and cheering. I got such a buzz off of that. That was just one of the best feelings; I lived for those moments. Even when something went wrong, I'd look over to him for his guidance. He'd be, like, 'Come on, get involved, get back… do this, do that…' I remember the amazing impact all this had on me and my development as a young footballer.

I was slight as a kid, so I used to get pushed off the ball. But then one day, rather than just letting it happen, I shrugged the player off me and shot a peach of a shot into the top corner. Naturally, I looked straight over to my dad. I remember seeing him on the side going mental with joy. He was clapping and shouting: 'That's it, Bill, that's what you've got to do.' And I knew there and then what I needed to do to succeed and win. It totally changed the way I played football. I became competitive. I saw that you have to… well, not actually *fight*, but you have to want the ball and I did.

Even when I started playing semi-professional football, Dad still came to watch me. His presence made all the difference. I realised that, on the occasions he didn't

come and watch, I often wouldn't play as well because there was no one for me to play in front of. My dad was my crowd, my inspiration. He was the person I wanted to impress. After the game I'd look forward to him telling me how I played, how it went.

He knew what he was chatting about. He had played for Tottenham when he was younger. He came through the youths and played for England schoolboys, but his parents said he had to go and work on a fruit and veg stall to earn money for the family. They were quite poor, so he had to give up football.

He had been a good player in his day, so I always took what he said about the game, and his advice and criticisms, very seriously. I'd take them on board. Sometimes people are against parents who encourage their kids from the touchline. But I was happy to have him shouting; for me, it was totally positive. It depends on the parents, I suppose. He was not one who would ever get involved with the manager – the decisions. He'd never abuse the referee or call out other players.

So if I was being lazy, he'd yell: 'Come on, get working, get working...' Or he'd

tell me to get more width. It wasn't criticism, it was coaching.

So I thought it was all positive, but I know there is a very thin line between that and those parents who overstep the mark and shout at players who aren't their children and at coaches and referees. Some parents don't know where to draw the line. No kid should be shouted at from a young age, particularly from dads who aren't qualified coaches. Who is that going to help?

For me, there were other guiding hands. My cousin Greg was a big inspiration to me. He was at Arsenal at the time. He'd even represented his country, turning out for England schoolboys. I used to play football at a cricket club and I could watch him train from there. He is four years older than me, so naturally as a kid I looked up to him. Talk about tekkers – he had loads of skills, tricks and tekk-nique. Greg could do a thousand kick-ups with a tennis ball. One thousand! With a tennis ball! He was only 13-years-old at the time. I'd watch him pulling that stuff out of the bag and I'd think: 'I want to get to that level.'

GET THE SKILLS:
NO-LOOK PASS

FACT FILE

ORIGIN: UNKNOWN
SKILL TYPE: PASS/CROSS
DIFFICULTY RATING: 5
TEKKERS RATING: 8
FREQUENTLY USED BY: RONALDINHO, CRISTIANO RONALDO, THIERRY HENRY, MICHAEL LAUDRUP

Billy: The first rule of tekkers is: if it's good enough for Ronaldinho, then it's good enough for anyone. And Ronaldinho loves a no-look pass. Nail one and you're a king. Mess one up and, well, the crowd won't let you forget it in a hurry.

The key is to move your head away only as you strike the ball, not a moment before. This is high-risk tekkers, but it's all about looking good. Or in this case, no-looking good.

APPROACH THE BALL FROM THE SIDE

AS YOU SWING YOUR STRIKING LEG LOOK AWAY FROM THE BALL

KEEP YOUR HEAD STILL AS YOU FOLLOW THROUGH WITH YOUR FOOT

FOLLOW THROUGH WITH YOUR FOOT UNTIL YOUR KICKING LEG IS STRAIGHT

APPROACH THE BALL FROM THE SIDE

AS YOU SWING YOUR STRIKING LEG LOOK AWAY FROM THE BALL

MESUT ÖZIL

'HE'S NOT ONE OF THEM BALLERS THAT WILL CLOWN ABOUT AND GIVE AWAY POSSESSION.'

MESUT ÖZIL

SPEED:	9
VISION:	10
TOUCH:	9
FINISHING:	9
TEKKERS:	9

F2 TRUMPS

Billy: D'you know what? Even as a Spurs fan I've got to admit that Özil is a quality baller. His swaz is off the scale.

Jez: No doubt. His vision and awareness are from another planet. There's 22 players on the pitch but there are things that only Mes can see. He's gotta be a striker's dream with that vision and with his ability to tap the perfect ball through…

Billy: So how come Giroud ain't banging in 40 goals a season if the service is so class?

Jez: Pipe down, Spurs boy, you can't blame Mes if Oli G ain't slotting 'em in every time! But listen, you know Özil used to practise for nine hours a day as a kid? Nine hours a day? That's proper dedication – it's crazily good.

Billy: Yep, you can have all the natural talent you like, working on it's still gonna take you to another level. So, come on, then, as a Gooner, what's your favourite Mesut assist?

Jez: Thing is, it's not just his assists. It's when he leaves a defender on his backside with one twist; when it's the middle of a crazy game and he slows down the pace and buys himself all the time in the world. He's a flipping magician! I remember one assist against Villa, though; there was a long ball played out from the back, and without even moving, he's stuck out his peg and back-heeled it on to Giroud and sent him clear to slot it in.

Billy: Unreal.

Jez: And what about at Anfield when he got that cross field pass and just killed it dead with one touch? Mate, even the Liverpool fans went quiet when that happened!

Billy: The thing is, before we met him, I thought he was going to be so shy. He comes across that way on the pitch. But he's got a super-cool sense of humour, hasn't he?

Jez: It's true. When we did the 'How May I Assist You?' video he was quality. Passing you a toilet roll as you sat on the loo. It's not every player who's gonna be up for pranks like that.

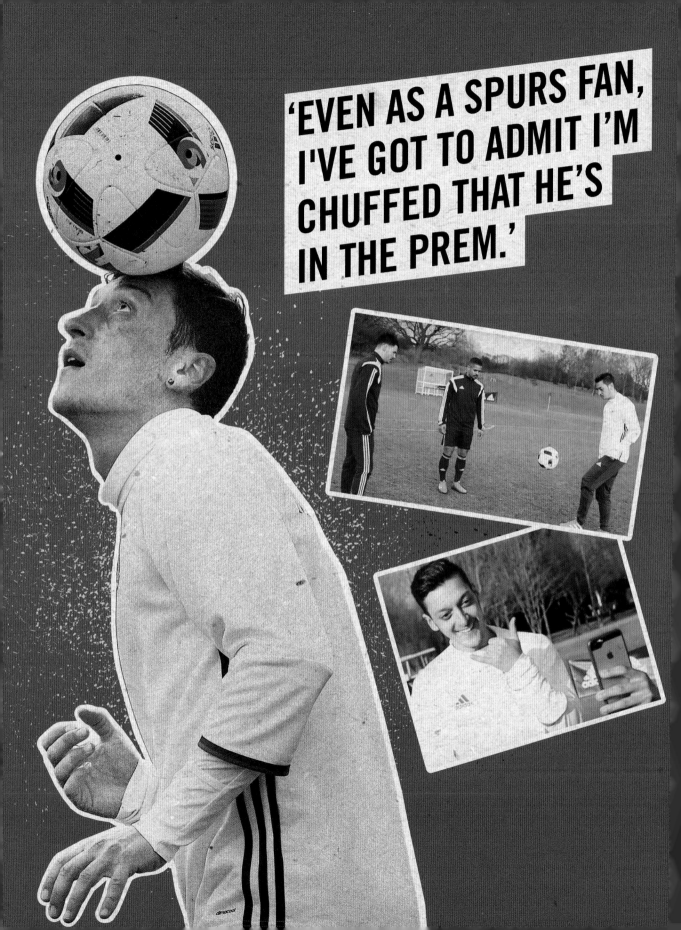

'EVEN AS A SPURS FAN, I'VE GOT TO ADMIT I'M CHUFFED THAT HE'S IN THE PREM.'

Mesut Özil

How May I Assist You?

Billy: Enough of the toilet chat, Jez. Let's keep it clean and on the pitch. You know he's got all these tricks in his locker but he doesn't rock them out for the sake of it. If it's a simple pass that's needed for his team to keep possession, he'll play the simple pass all day long. He's not one of them ballers that will clown about and give away possession. Also, he makes the players around him look better than they are. He's got that selfless streak.

Jez: That's right, he's a serious guy, not a show-off. He'd rather assist than score. Even if he sees the chance for glory, he'll offer it up on a plate for his team-mate… Wow, it must be something else to play with that guy.

Billy: It's amazing enough just to watch him! He's the sort of player you want to focus on all the time, even when he's not on the ball. That's when you notice his full range of class. He glides around, actually it's more like he's skating, and he finds these little pockets of space. All on the quiet – he's

like a ninja! Even as a Spurs fan, I've got to admit I'm chuffed that he's in the Prem.

Jez: Come on, this isn't even about which club he plays for. He's world class, simple as. He's won the World Cup, he was the assist king at Real Madrid…

Billy: All right, all right; tell me this, then, if he's so top quality, then why did Real let him go to Arsenal? If you're Madrid, you don't let a top player slip through your fingers, do you?

Jez: Mate, don't listen to me, listen to Cristiano Ronaldo. He proper kicked off when Real sold Mesut! You're telling me Ronaldo doesn't know what he's chatting about? He rates him, José Mourinho rates him, Wenger rates him, Joachim Löw rates him… you want me to go on, or you want to hold your hands up?

Billy: I rate him too! Calm down, son, I reeled you in big style there!

DESIGN YOUR OWN BALL

(AND SEE IT COME ALIVE)

CHAPTER TWO

THE F2 STORY:
ORIGINS: JEZ

Jez: One of my earliest memories is the day my parents got me a sponge football. I must have been two or three. I loved that sponge football! I started kicking it around the house right away. I had barely learned how to walk at this stage, but all I wanted to do was kick the ball. A little further down the line, I got told off because I had a size four, leather ball and my mum used to tell me all the time to use the sponge ball instead. She'd say: 'You're going to break something one day!'

They were great parents. My dad wanted me to do well in football. A lot of dads want that for their sons, don't they? But, listen, my dad really motivated me. He used to take me to the local park from a young age, with my brother. He'd teach us skills and do various drills: passing, shooting, control. He was serious about making this work. It wasn't pressure, he just wanted to give me the best chance.

He was a clever guy. He knew just how to get to me. While we were out in the park he'd be watching me like hawk. He'd say: 'If you want to make it in this game you're going to have to do a lot better than that.' He used to drive me on and on, but he was right. He knew that I responded best to him when he ignited my competitive nature.

If he felt he had to bend reality a bit to get that going, he was willing to do it. It was all to an honest end. He might say to me: 'I've seen this kid at the Arsenal academy and I think he's slightly better than you.' Ha! He knew exactly what he was doing! I don't even know if he had seen such a kid; he might well have been telling a porkie. But he knew it would make me work harder. It was worth it. And I became quite curious about this fabled kid Dad had seen. I remember one time going along to see the Arsenal under-12s play a game against Chelsea.

'I HAD BARELY LEARNED TO WALK ... BUT ALL I WANTED TO DO WAS KICK THE BALL.'

I was peeking through a bush to watch it because it was a behind-closed-doors game. I was thinking, I was sure they'd be much better than this – my dad made out they were much better! That gave me a new confidence boost. I realised that, comparatively, I was at a better level than I thought I was. I was on a par or maybe even better than these guys. I saw nothing that I couldn't do as well or better myself.

I was buzzing.

So I used to practise every day. I kept a log of how many hours I put in each day, week, month and year. It was a calendar. I had different coloured pens to represent different tekkers. It worked so efficiently that I'd be able to take one look at it and compare across different time-frames. The log seemed to take me, an already determined and competitive

kid, to another level. I'd end up practising on Christmas Day. I was a dedicated kid. I saw playing at Christmas as a chance to push myself ahead of the competition who might not be out that day. This was what I was all about between the ages of 11 and 14.

I believe in God. I'm a Christian, I was brought up in a Christian family and went to a private Christian school in Hackney.

My brother went there, too, and my sisters. My mum was the head teacher and my grandfather had been a pastor. He was one of the founders of the school. I got straight As. There was no playground, which made it difficult to polish my football skills. So I had to make sure that when I got home, I practised. I had the dedication to make sure that's what I did. That's partly why I kept the log.

'I COULDN'T BELIEVE THE WHOLE EXPERIENCE; THE DIFFERENCE BETWEEN SEEING A MATCH LIVE AT THE GROUND AND WATCHING IT ON TELEVISION.'

So we were a tight family unit. My dad would give me challenges. He'd say: 'This week, I only want you to use your left foot.' This included not only practice but while I was playing games. I don't think he'd think I was about to go through with it, but I did! It was like a boot camp for my left foot. And, since then, I've always been fairly comfortable with my weak side.

I remember seeing a game at Arsenal. I can't remember who it was against. Wenger was the manager and it was at Highbury. I was just a little kid. But I'd had to wait a while because my parents didn't have much money – certainly not enough to just be splashing out on match tickets left, right and centre. Ray Lee, who used to play for Arsenal, had taken me under his wing and coached me. It was Ray that got me tickets for Arsenal. I couldn't believe the whole experience; the difference between seeing a match live at the ground and watching it on television.

Observing players in the flesh was unbelievable. Now I work with top players and it doesn't phase me. But when I was that kid, I'd never seen a player in real life. Then I suddenly see them all at once. It was just fascinating. I'd seen them on television and now suddenly they were right there, getting off the coach just yards away from me, warming up and then playing. I could not believe

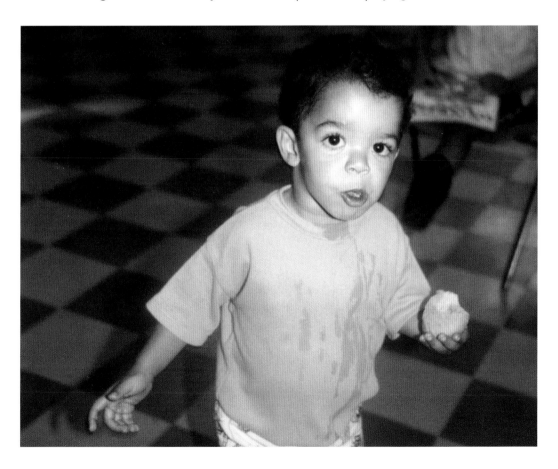

it. Watching them play live was just a brilliant experience, I loved it.

It made me think how far I might go as a pro. You know, I still maintain that Bill and me could slip in at a high level. Our fitness may not be quite elite level but only because it doesn't have to be. If we got fit, we could do it. Every pro we've played with has said we could fit in, technically, at the highest level. Which is nice to hear.

Whether you make it in the first place comes down to favouritism sometimes, too. It can be about who you know and whether a coach likes you or not. At many clubs I've been to, I have seen certain boys who, for one reason or another, have been favoured by the coaches. It's just the nature of the beast; you've got to go with the flow.

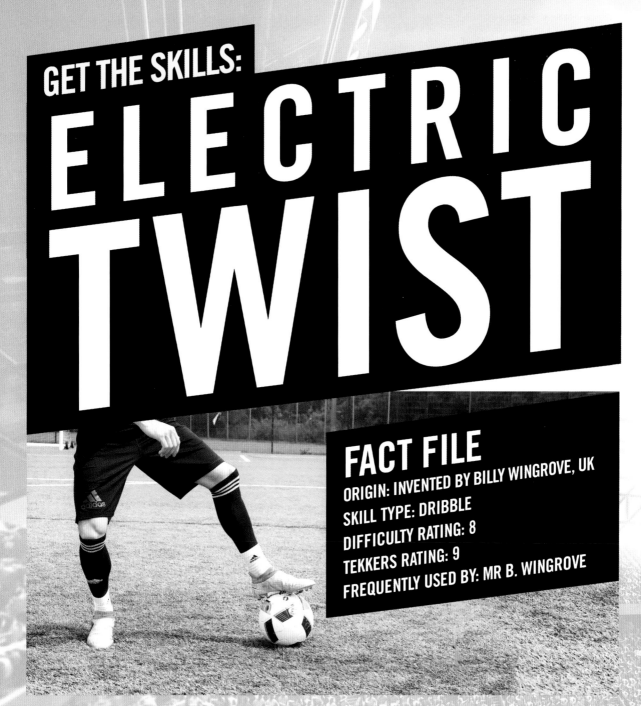

GET THE SKILLS:
ELECTRIC TWIST

FACT FILE
ORIGIN: INVENTED BY BILLY WINGROVE, UK
SKILL TYPE: DRIBBLE
DIFFICULTY RATING: 8
TEKKERS RATING: 9
FREQUENTLY USED BY: MR B. WINGROVE

Billy: Now you see me, now you don't. Here's how you take your skills to the next level and leave your opponent with twisted blood.

Essentially it's a step-over, followed by a feint, drag-back and twist into open space. Start off practising slowly, break the move down into parts and master each section, before quickening it up and then trying it on in a game.

It's perfect for taking a defender out of the game. Just as they think you're going one way, bang, you spin out and sprint off in the other direction. Electric.

STEP OVER THE BALL WITH YOUR WEAKER FOOT

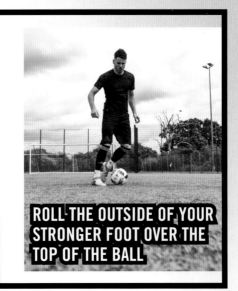

ROLL THE OUTSIDE OF YOUR STRONGER FOOT OVER THE TOP OF THE BALL

DRAG BACK WITH THE SOLE OF YOUR BOOT...

... AND TWIST AT THE SAME TIME

ACCELERATE AWAY

STEP OVER...

ROLL FOOT ON TOP OF BALL

DRAG...

...AND TWIST AT THE SAME TIME

ACCELERATE AWAY

CRISTIANO
RONALDO

'WE'VE GOT SPECIAL LOVE FOR RONALDO. HE'S SO MISUNDERSTOOD.'

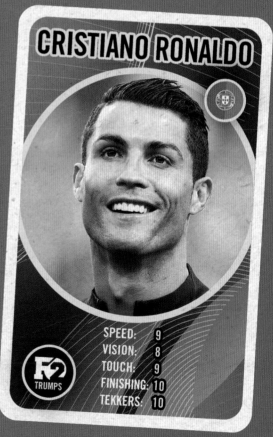

CRISTIANO RONALDO

SPEED:	9
VISION:	8
TOUCH:	9
FINISHING:	10
TEKKERS:	10

F2 TRUMPS

Jez: This guy, I believe he is one of the most misunderstood men in football. We've met him more than once and I can tell you he is so nice and so genuine.

Billy: One hundred per cent. Ronaldo's a top guy.

Jez: I don't know why people think he's arrogant. Maybe because on the pitch he doesn't apologise for who he is? But look at his lifestyle and who he really is. I think he's supremely confident and there's obviously a thin line, which could be easily mistaken for arrogance, but of all the players we've worked with he's one of the nicest. So down to earth.

Billy: People need to become more aware that most footballers are really solid, decent people. The media can be negative about footballers sometimes but our experiences of them are really positive.

Jez: Even the biggest names.

Billy: Especially the biggest names. It's a funny thing but I've often found that the bigger the name, the more down-to-earth they are. Maybe the top stars feel they have less to prove.

Jez: When we worked with him on a shoot, Ronaldo had time for us and everyone on the shoot. The man was full of respect. We've encountered him personally a few times and I've never seen him being arrogant. We've got special love for Ronaldo. He's so misunderstood.

Billy: So let's just celebrate his footballing genius for a while.

Jez: He's got so much in his locker. How do you pick out one of his tricks to highlight? He's got chop tekkers, the scissor, the

knuckleball. That dip! He's also a lot faster than people sometimes realise.

Billy: His free kicks are lethal. How many times have we seen opposition players and fans drop their heads when they concede

‘SO WHAT IF HE TAKES CARE OF THE WAY HE LOOKS? HE TAKES A WHOLE LOAD MORE CARE OVER HOW HE PLAYS.’

Messi VS Ronaldo

a free kick to a Ronaldo team? It's like they feel they've already conceded a goal before he even steps up to take it!

But he's about so much more than free kicks. Over the years he's become more effective at headers.

Jez: For sure, his career has evolved. He started on the right wing, moved to the left and has since played much further forward and more centrally. Wherever he is, he's a game changer.

Billy: Even when he's not on the pitch he can influence a game. In the Euro 2016 final he was there on the touchline, bellowing, pointing and encouraging after he had to go off injured. It doesn't take anything away from the 11 Portuguese players on the pitch to say that he was having an effect.

Jez: And that match, right there, was the one that put the icing on the cake of his

career to date. To win something with your country must be an unbelievable honour!

Billy: How cool has it been to watch Ronaldo and Messi battle it out in La Liga over the years? I can't think of any two-man rivalry that has been such a treat. They've both scored in two Uefa Champions League finals and have both broken the 50-goal barrier in a single season.

You can go around and around on who is best. It's like the Ayrton Senna v Alain Prost rivalry in F1. Or the Björn Borg v John McEnroe rivalry in tennis. I say, Who cares which of the two is best? Just enjoy both of them!

Jez: The man himself has said that the rivalry has driven him on to become better and better. That's good enough for me. I just want to enjoy the remainder of their respective careers. I don't go along with the criticism of Ronaldo, even over his appearance. So what if he takes care of the way he looks? He takes a whole load more care over how he plays. He's the man. We should treasure him.

DESIGN YOUR OWN KIT

(AND SHARE IT ONLINE)

F2 CHAPTER THREE

THE F2 STORY:
EARLY TEKKERS: BILLY

Billy: I used to go to the Arsenal training ground sometimes with my cousin Tommy, who played his games for the youths. For me just to be able to step into that environment and to hang out was amazing. George Graham was the manager and I remember one day I saw him walking towards the clubhouse. We were hanging around outside. I quickly got hold of a ball and started doing a few tricks outside the clubhouse, as nonchalantly as possible.

I really hoped he'd notice me. He did. As he walked past he said: 'We've got to sign him up, this young lad.' Even as a Spurs fan that was just an incredible moment. Because praise is important, isn't it? You need a balance of praise and constructive criticism. I'd advise anyone reading this who wants to crack on with football or freestyling to learn to listen to wise heads. My dad knew I loved all of his guidance – even the tougher words. Add in his footballing ability and the fact he played for Spurs and I was, like, 'Wow'. We're all Spurs fans in my family. I love them all.

The first Spurs game my dad took me to was Spurs v Coventry. I remember going into White Hart Lane, amazed by the atmosphere, the excitement and the noise. I wasn't intimidated by the volume and the crowds. I just loved it all, the full experience. I was about 11 years old. Me and my dad sat in the East Stand, right at the very back, at the top. When we scored my dad jumped up and spilt all his drink over me. But we lost the match 3-1. Dad was fuming! He'd paid about £160 all in and said: 'I'm not doing this again, it's not worth it.' I was so distraught when he said that. We didn't go to many games for a while. Spurs lost a lot of games back then, so it was impossible to predict which game to go to if you wanted to guarantee seeing a win.

We did go back though, and sometimes Spurs even won. One time, my dad put some money on a match against our local rivals, Arsenal. He should have listened to me. I told him: 'Dad, we're going to win it 2-1. Chris Armstrong is going to score the first goal, then Arsenal will equalise with Dennis Bergkamp, then Teddy Sheringham will get the winner.' I'd named the

I want to look the part. I choose shorts from Matalan, a baggy khaki pair with an unnecessary number of pockets. Then I find a T-shirt that someone gave me at work...

...nuts". I play safe with the trainers and pick my oldest, most comfortable and, quite frankly... malodorous pair. They...

...ing in the morning.
We chat as we walk along the Grand Union Canal underneath the Westway in search of a pitch, and Billy tells me he comes from a footballing...

...and Arsenal; his cousin Greg Lincoln currently turns out for Northampton Town after a spell, and two Champions' League games, for Arsenal. Billy himself had a trial with Spurs when he was 11, but he was considered too small. Undeterred, Billy played non-League...

...corner shop first

...ball up on the half-volley. As demonstrated on behalf of various corporate clients by Zinedine Zidane.
Mr Woo Lie on back, supporting your hips and moving legs in...

...feet. As seen on the T-Mobile advert with Korean freestyler Mr Woo. Extremely difficult to master.
The Wingrove push-up Billy's speciality. Balance the ball on the back of your neck and do press-ups. Visually impressive, but of limited applica... during matches.

...when in the next 10 minutes I fail to achieve a repeat.
When I leave him, Billy is lying full-length under...

...train rumbles past way into Paddington, and ...trians stop to watch. Still he waves goodbye, lo... like the happiest young... the world.

For more details of Billy Wingrove's career:
www.billywingrove.co.uk

'YOU NEED A BALANCE OF PRAISE AND CONSTRUCTIVE CRITICISM.'

Roaldinho 10.

Billy's on the ball

Football freestyler shows off his skills

LEARN FREESTYLE FOOTBALL

WITH THE UK'S NUMBER ONE **BILLY WINGROVE**

VOL 1

Spurs juggler happy to be a control freak

BY RAOUL SIMONS

MEET the Tottenham trickster. Inspired by a pre-sumo Diego Maradona, Billy "football freestyle" champion who has been livening up the half-time entertainment at White Hart Lane this season.

Parading around the pitch while juggling a ball with various parts of his anatomy, the 20-year-old — and others like him — have taken traditional "keepy-uppies" to a new level.

Football freestyle is now so popular there are countrywide competitions where players' expertly-crafted routines are judged in the same way as ice dancers or gymnasts.

Ever the innovators, Spurs have latched on to this growing pastime and given Wingrove a contract as the Premiership's first freestyle coach.

His duties not only involve the half-time show on matchdays, but also teaching youngsters new tricks through courses run as part of the club's community scheme.

...becomes a lot easier — and I've been practising all my life.

"Now all of a sudden it has become my job. When I was about 16 I entered a freestyle competi...

Foot perfect: Tottenham's Robbie Keane joins in as Billy Wingrove shows his skill

scoreline, the scorers and the sequence of goals – and they actually came in! But he didn't put a pound on my version. I always remember that. I literally couldn't believe it. He would have won a packet! But we beat Arsenal, so, happy days.

He liked the odd flutter here and there and sometimes that was to my advantage. One day he had a win on the horses. He said: 'Right, I'm going to buy you a Spurs kit.' This was my first: sky-blue. He bought me the full kit. I put it on there and then in the shop and wore it home. Seriously, I was the happiest person in the world. That's the good thing about growing up in a family without much money; you really appreciate those moments because they are rare.

After I left school, I played in local team East Herts College. I went on to join Ware, Enfield Town FC in the Ryman Prem at the time. That was all between the ages of 16 and 19. My intention originally was to become a professional footballer and ideally play for the mighty Spurs. I worked hard and learned what I could.

I had a lot of heroes. I really looked up to Gazza. The way he played was incredible. In his heyday, it always seemed like he was happy and having a laugh. And to be so good at football but also be so bubbly – that was the sort of player and person I wanted to be.

It was sad to see how things got darker for him. I met him once. He wasn't

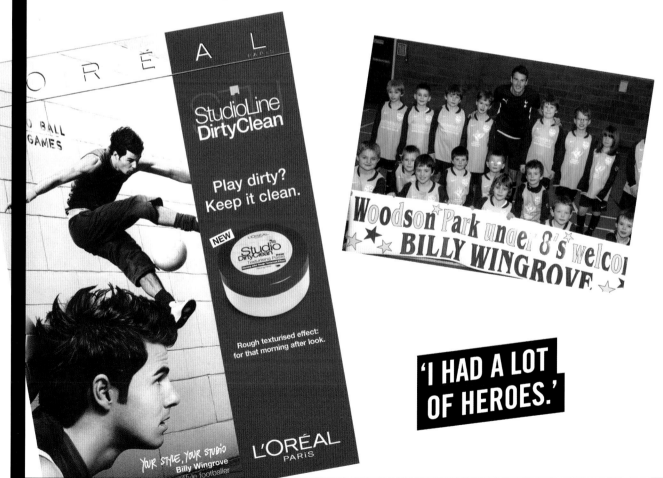

O R É A L
PARIS

O BALL
GAMES

StudioLine
DirtyClean

Play dirty?
Keep it clean.

NEW
Studio
DirtyClean
Texturising Paste

Rough texturised effect:
for that morning after look.

YOUR STYLE, YOUR STUDIO
Billy Wingrove
freestyle footballer

L'ORÉAL
PARIS

www.lorealdirtyclean.com

Woodson Park under 8's welcol
★ ★ BILLY WINGROVE ★ →

'I HAD A LOT OF HEROES.'

in the best form. It's such a shame that his addictions got the better of him. Perhaps he wasn't guided in the right way following his injuries and after his playing career ended. But at his peak, he was a global footballing superstar, living the dream. His skill, flair and self-expression were unbelievable. I wanted to be that type of player. A player who changes the game, the match winner. Like Gareth Bale was later for Spurs. That sort of star.

Gazza was so vulnerable and open as a player. There was nothing behind the curtains. You could see how much football meant to him and how ready he was to take the responsibility on his shoulders. I see the same with Bale. He steps up and wins the game for the team.

I had more heroes as time went on. A lot were Spurs players but there were others from different teams, such as Ian Wright of Arsenal and Eric Cantona of Manchester United. Wrighty was so raw, like a street player. I understood him, because I played in the streets at the time. He was an electric player and he meant so much to me, even as a player for the bitter rivals of my beloved Spurs. As for Cantona, how could I not love him? He was the coolest, most composed foreign player. I like personalities, I really do.

Gianfranco Zola was another player I liked, partly because, like him, I was small. I was actually the smallest kid in my year.

'SOMETIMES, WHEN YOU HAVE A VISION, NOT EVERYONE WILL SEE IT.'

No one took me at all seriously – they called me Little Bill. But I didn't want to be Little Bill, I wanted to be a serious footballer. So I admired Zola because he was that small guy who broke through and made it. I took a lot of encouragement from him.

But my ultimate hero when I was growing up was Ronaldinho. The way he expresses himself with a football is second to none. I've never seen a player play with such freedom. For me he is the best and always will be.

I ended up bowing out of my playing career aged 19. By then I had been trying my luck at freestyling and decided I wanted to take that path. It was partly about the quest for excellence: I saw myself as much closer to becoming the best in the world at freestyle than at football. It was a career move. It was also the biggest sacrifice of my life. To stand

up and say, 'For the next seven years, I'm not going to play professional football,' was massive. By this stage, Stevenage were interested in signing me. There were options. But I looked at it in career terms: how much money would I make at Stevenage? What prospects were there? What would happen if I got injured? How many kids would I have inspired playing for Stevenage? We're enthusing people around the world with The F2 and, with all due respect to Stevenage, I wasn't likely to get an international platform there.

It was a huge decision. The biggest decision of my life. My mum, best interests at heart, said she didn't want me to pursue a career doing the tricks. At that time football freestyling as a business didn't even exist. So, with that in mind, she wanted me to go and work at the Tesco down the road. She felt the tricks route was too risky. 'Juggling a football isn't a career path,' she

said. I knew she was saying it out of love, but I saw that there was a career path. I had a clear vision for it. Sometimes, when you have a vision, not everyone will see it. Make no mistake; I was under a lot of pressure from my parents to get a 'real' job.

When I finally decided to dedicate myself to freestyling, I was still playing for Ware town. I was getting paid the most in the team and really enjoying it. I scored 17 goals from left midfield. I was doing really well. One day, we played Clapton and their right-back injured me. He'd been having a proper row with a team-mate of mine. They'd been in each other's faces a lot. A while later in the game I went in for a 50/50 tackle with this guy. He snapped all of my ligaments, on both sides of my ankles. The injury was so bad. The physio said: 'You'd have been better off clean snapping your ankle because the rehab is

going to be so bad.' Gutting!

I came back after six months. That was a long time to be out and my return actually maybe came a little too soon. I had the same injury again and was out for three more months. It was so frustrating. Almost unbelievable. When I came back a second time I was too scared to go in for tackles. I wasn't the same player. I'd been head-and-shoulders above everyone before the injury but now… not so much.

Soon after my return, I got a slight knock again and I decided to focus on the tricks. But this is not a hard luck story. It was a great decision and maybe all those injury problems were just life showing me what I was meant to do. More freestyling work was coming in, the money was going up and I was getting better and better jobs.

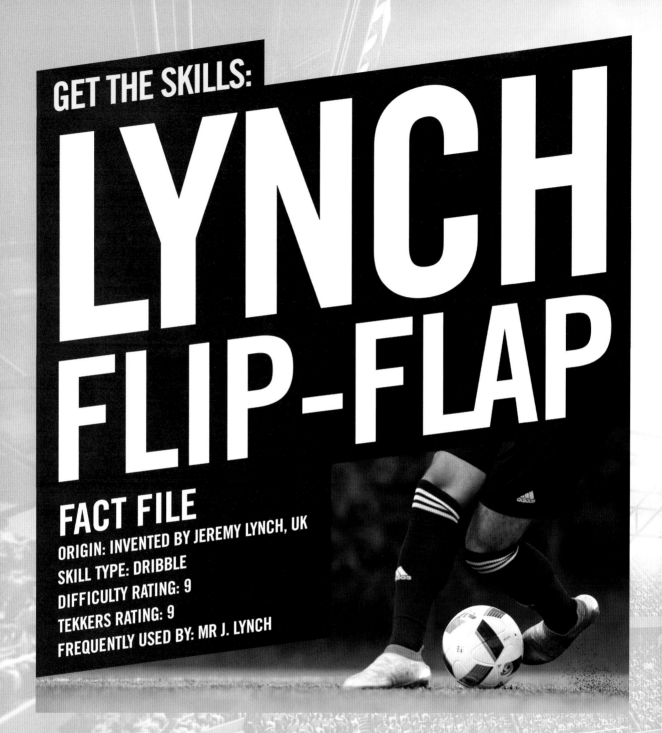

GET THE SKILLS:
LYNCH FLIP-FLAP

FACT FILE

ORIGIN: INVENTED BY JEREMY LYNCH, UK

SKILL TYPE: DRIBBLE

DIFFICULTY RATING: 9

TEKKERS RATING: 9

FREQUENTLY USED BY: MR J. LYNCH

Jez: You've heard of the flip-flap, right? Well this takes things up a level. It's a great dribbling skill, with an equally great name. I wonder where that came from?

Approach the defender face on, then simply step over the ball, while tapping it forward with your trailing leg. Then quickly flip your standing foot outwards to take the ball wide of your man. You'll be past him before he can say Zlatan Ibrahimovic. Or in this case, Jeremy Lynch.

APPROACH THE DEFENDER

STEP OVER THE BALL

TAP THE BALL FORWARD WITH
YOUR TRAILING FOOT

USE THE OUTSIDE OF YOUR
STANDING FOOT TO BEAT YOUR MAN

...AND ACCELERATE AWAY...

...LEAVING THE DEFENDER ROASTED

BOOSH!!!

LIONEL MESSI

'JUST TO BE IN HIS PRESENCE, TO TALK WITH HIM, KICK A BALL WITH HIM, WAS UNBELIEVABLE.'

LIONEL MESSI

SPEED:	9
VISION:	9
TOUCH:	10
FINISHING:	10
TEKKERS:	9

F2 TRUMPS

Jez: Messi's Messi, isn't he? He's just one of – if not the – greatest ever. I still can't believe we met him. Just to be in his presence, to talk with him, kick a ball with him, was unbelievable. When we jetted off to La Masia, the Barcelona training ground, we were so excited. To be honest, it was mad enough that he already knew who we were!

Billy: I was cheeky on the day. I'd heard that the Barcelona team motto is to always be prepared to receive the ball, come what may. To test this out, I pinged him the ball while he was on the phone. He only had a second's notice but he casually killed the ball dead! He's amazing. If you asked me who is the best player in the world it would be a super-close run thing between him and Ronaldo. But for me, Messi would probably edge it. So let's break it down – why is he so good?

Jez: For a start, he keeps the ball *so* close to his feet, to keep control of it at all times. This sounds obvious and simple on paper, but when I say he keeps the ball close to his feet I mean *close*.

Billy: It's as if it's glued to them. Another Messi classic is to beat his opponent with the shoulder drop. That's classic Messi, isn't it?

Jez: Yep, he runs at defenders and forces them to commit. That's when he makes his move – attacking space with his first touch. It must make them nervous as anything! And sometimes he'll cut inside. Defenders know he'll do that but, as the man told me himself, that knowledge in itself is not enough to stop him. He told me: 'It's not if – it's when.' So there's a lesson for us all – get your timing right and leave your opponent chasing your shadow.

Billy: La Liga's got its fair share of assist machines but Messi's killer passes seem to be in a league of their own. He uses the inside of

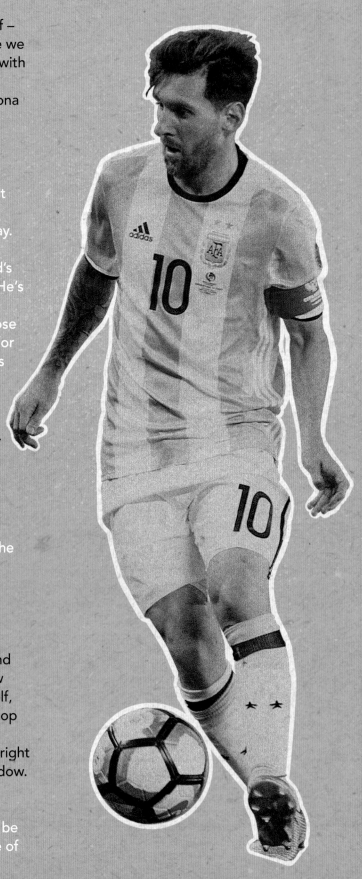

his foot to get a bit of curl into the ball and sends it into that corridor of uncertainty. Deadly and tantalising.

Jez: He uses the inside of his foot on free kicks, too. He's looking for placement rather than power when he sends it in. Time after time you'll see him send it over the wall so it dips down into the near post. Watch him from the start: he prepares for the free kick side-on from the ball. Everything is special. For me, Messi is the best passer in the world, but he's so good at everything else that it gets overlooked!

Billy: How do you even begin to pick out the top Messi moments on the pitch? There are so many of them. At 19 years old he scored a hat-trick against Real Madrid, defining the game even at that age. Barca were down to ten men at the time, but he unleashed a left-foot shot across the keeper. No chance!

Jez: Yeah, I also remember his winner against Iran in the 2014 World Cup. The Iranians had held on so well to get an unlikely point and then, right at the end, in injury time, he just dipped his left foot and curled the ball home. What can you do with that? It's a privilege to live in the same era as the man. I want to do more video shoots with Messi. I really want that.

'IT'S A PRIVILEGE TO LIVE IN THE SAME ERA AS THE MAN.'

A FEW OF OUR FAVOURITE THINGS

BILLY

Favourite goal: Gazza's free kick in the 1991 FA Cup semi-final against Arsenal just leaps out, doesn't it? He was 35 yards out! It's outrageous for anyone to even attempt a shot from that distance; to actually get it in in the top corner is mad. It looked like his team-mates were half thinking he was going to cross it to them. But instead he arrowed a free kick into the top corner past David Seaman.

I remember running out of my house to celebrate. I was going crazy. The television commentary for that goal was great, too: 'Is Gascoigne going to have a crack? He is, you know... Oh, I say!' Happy times.

Favourite match: the 4-4 draw with Arsenal in 2008. I loved the drama – David Bentley's 40-yard goal, the way the score line went back and forth and Aaron Lennon's injury-time equaliser. What a fight back!

Favourite England international: you know I could say Gazza again. I don't want to keep saying Gazza, but he is without doubt my favourite England

international of all time. So I'm saying just that – Gazza.'

Favourite overseas club: hmm… it's between Barca and Real Madrid, isn't it? I love watching them both play. Jez will say Barca, I reckon, so I'll say Real Madrid – we always do that, choose one each. I think everything about the club, even their kit, is absolutely amazing. The size and structure of the club is absolutely monumental. They always attract the best players. The history.

Favourite international tournament: I loved the 2006 World Cup, partly because I was there. Right up to Italy's penalty shoot-out win, the whole tournament was entertaining.

Favourite sportsman from another sport: Lewis Hamilton. I don't watch F1 but I've met him and I've so much admiration for how much he always wants to win. He's prepared to risk his life to win. And, like so many top sports stars, he's actually such a down-to-earth and humble guy.

Favourite food: you can't beat a bit of Nando's. I have half-chicken (either lemon and herb or hot; I never go medium). On the side I have peri peri chips, corn on the cob, one soft drink and one cake. On the plate I mix together half wild-herb sauce, half garlic sauce and then I shave the corn with a knife and mix it up with the sauce. I recommend it to anyone. That's my top Nando's tip. Try it and thank me later. Jez and me actually had a Nando's Black Card for two years, so we had free meals. I don't know if they knew what they were letting themselves in for – we went there all the time! We started going every single night.

Favourite TV show: *Game of Thrones*. Favourite character is Khaleesi – for the obvious reasons…

Favourite catchphrase: love, peace and tekkers. It sums up The F2: it's about love, peace and technical ability. That's all you need, isn't it?

Favourite pop star: I really like Ed Sheeran. He's got some relaxing tracks that are right up my street. Our job is quite hectic, so to chill out in the bath and listen to him is great. The guy is a genius. Favourite songs are the mellow ones: 'Tenerife Sea' and 'Photograph'. The really chilled-out ones. Before a show we listen to some sort of grime or rap to get us going. But, otherwise, whoever the artist is, I like songs that slow the pace of life down a bit.

Favourite season: summer, all day long. I love the heat. It makes me happy in the morning.

Favourite drink: I'll say Appletiser. It's one of the healthier fizzy drinks so hopefully I'm not being naughty by suggesting a fizzy drink.

Favourite snack: healthy eating is important but you can still have the odd treat. And I do like crisps. Salt and vinegar Chipsticks or steak McCoy's. But I go round in circles, preferring different ones all the time.

A FEW OF OUR FAVOURITE THINGS

JEZ

Favourite goal: Dennis Bergkamp's wonder strike against Newcastle in 2002. Such a cheeky approach – peel-and-swivel magic. That first touch, though. Just gorgeous. I love that goal. I also love some of Cristiano Ronaldo's knuckle balls into the top corner. Boosh!

Favourite match: I'll say AC Milan v Liverpool in the 2005 Champions League final. Regardless of who you support, from an English point of view that match was huge. That match stands out in the modern era. Look, you may not believe this, but when Liverpool were 3-0 down at half-time I actually said: 'You never know, they could turn this round.' Honestly, I did! And then they did! Wow. Imagine being a Liverpool fan that night, what it must have felt like for them. Now imagine being a Liverpool fan at the ground that night. An unreal evening, one no football fan who saw it will forget.

Favourite manager: José Mourinho. I love characters in football. I think

it's great for the game. Zlatan, Balotelli, Mourinho. I don't agree with everything they do, but personality is good. Some footballers have it all sapped out of them through media training. Well, that has its place I suppose, but I'll always love a character. Even if they make our rivals stronger. Maybe it's because we're entertainers that I love it so much.

Favourite England international: Ashley Cole. This may be a surprising choice. I think he's faced a lot of criticism and misunderstanding over the years. But, listen, very few players who play for England can say that, for a significant period of time, they were the best on the planet in their position. During his time for England, Ashley was our most consistent player and he doesn't get enough credit for that.

Favourite overseas club: Barca. They are the best in the world. They've dominated the scene for the last decade. Everyone in this generation is privileged to see Messi. And Ronaldo at Real Madrid. The two greatest players, locking horns over and over. Only when they retire will people realise what we had. Will there be another Messi and Ronaldo? Some people say, 'Yes,' but I'm not so sure.

Favourite international tournament: I'll go with Euro 2016 because Adidas flew us over and let us watch lots of the games. To experience it first-hand was ace. It got criticised a lot as a tournament but it wasn't as bad as people made out. There was some great football.

Favourite sportsman from another sport: that's a toughie, man. I'll say Lewis Hamilton, too. He's massive. I'm an F1 fan, a keen go-karter too. I've got the third fastest track time at my local course. I'll be working on that – I want first place!

Favourite food: sweet potato. In any form – chips, wedges, mash. I have it nearly every day. It's healthy, too. Yeah, man, I love it.

Favourite singer: Carrie Underwood or Jazmine Sullivan. As she's closer to home, I'll go with Jazmine Sullivan.

Favourite season: I'm all about summer, too. So different to the winter, when we've actually made ourselves ill practising our tekkers outdoors all day.

Favourite drink: I like water and lime: simple, healthy, good.

Favourite snack: salt and vinegar baked crisps.

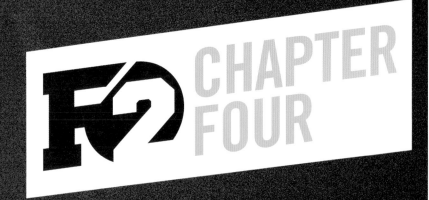

JEZ'S GOT TALENT

Jez: I was on Arsenal's books for a while as a kid, which, as a Gunners fan, was unreal. But it didn't last long. I'll always remember the day they let me go. I was given the news by a representative at the club called Roy Massey. He was very good about it, to be honest. It can't have been easy telling kids their dreams weren't going to come true, but part of his job description was to let players know when they were being let go. He told me it was over and said to me: 'We've got links with Colchester if you want to give it a go with them. You should definitely be playing at an academy.'

It turned out that Liam Brady had made the final decision. In case you haven't heard of Liam, he was a majorly gifted midfielder for Arsenal and Juventus back in the 1970s and 1980s. He was famed throughout the game for his sweet left foot, razor-sharp vision and graceful passing. By the time I came under his watch, he was head of youth development at Arsenal. So he got the final say on kids. Apparently, the other coaches at the club wanted me to stay. But Brady thought I was too raw and that I needed more coaching. To be fair, my football understanding was probably not what it could be. They told me that, on the ball, I was probably the best at the club across the board. They said: 'We can't fault you there.' But off the ball I

'THE MORE TIME WENT ON, THE MORE MY DESTINY WAS BECOMING CLEAR.'

was probably one of the worst.

I hadn't had any coaching. I was a very raw player when I went there. It was just technique that let me down. If they had taken the time to coach me then I've no doubt I would have made it to the first team. There were a couple of runs I should have made that I didn't. That was that. But he was right at the time. I've got to respect his decision. I have absolutely no grudge against him at all.

I held it together when Massey told me the bad news – just. But as soon as I was in the car with my mum, I burst into tears. At the time I couldn't understand it. But now it's so clear – I was meant to do something arguably bigger and more far-reaching than being another professional footballer. Bill and me are the only people on the planet doing exactly what we're doing, but there are thousands and thousands of footballers.

What we've done over these last few years is even better than being a career footballer. And we get to meet and work with the top names in a way that is unique. So I feel pretty blessed. Looking back, I wouldn't have had it any other way. If I'd have made it at Arsenal there would be no The F2. Now, that would be a true tragedy!

There have been other opportunities along the way. I got offered a trial at Fulham as a teenager. But I turned it down because it felt wrong to put my mum through all the travel. It would have been a four-hour round trip for her, what with rush-hour traffic, because we were living in east London. She took me everywhere as a kid – the legend she was.

'I WAS ALWAYS SERIOUS ABOUT WINNING.'

So I wasn't about to put her through that on a regular basis.

The more time went on, the more my destiny was becoming clear. But there were setbacks and potential diversions. As a kid I used to watch *X Factor*. The ups and downs and twists of it used to interest me. It's hard not to get caught up in the drama of it all, isn't it? For me, the star of the show was probably not the contestants but the head judge, Simon Cowell. I enjoyed his directness. So when he started up a new series, *Britain's Got Talent*, I got to thinking. The *X Factor* was all about singing, but *BGT* was open to everyone from comedians to dancers with dogs, you name it. As I watched the first series, I wondered if I could find a place in it with my football tricks.

I was very confident with my tricks by this stage. I knew what my value was. And I knew I'd stand out on the show, because there was no football on it. So I decided to enter the second series. I posted off the form and waited for the audition day. There was a long queue on the first day. As I waited, I looked around the other contestants: it was a totally mixed bag. I saw the most crazy people there, I really did. Clowns, dancers, kids – there were really vivid colours in the queue. It was just a real array, almost like a celebration of talent. Some were there more for the experience than to compete. Me? I was always serious about winning.

GET THE SKILLS:
NEYMAR
TOUCH TEKKERS

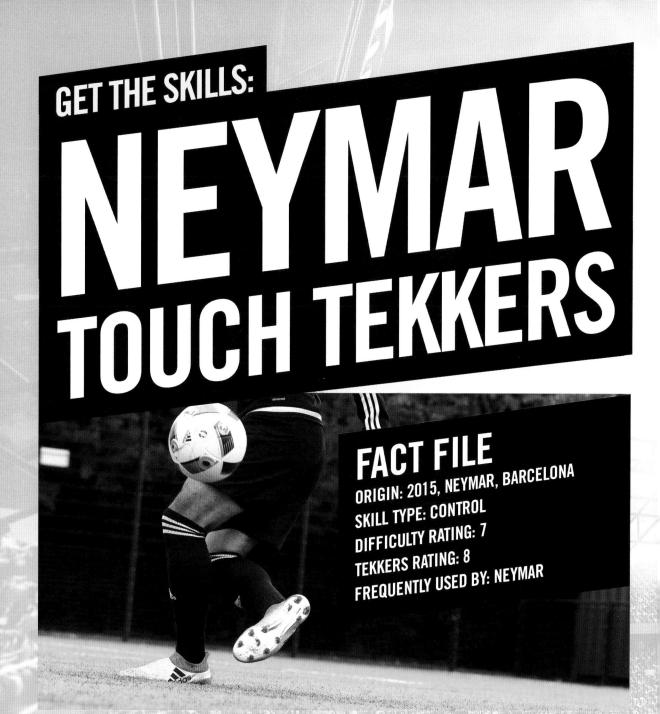

FACT FILE
ORIGIN: 2015, NEYMAR, BARCELONA
SKILL TYPE: CONTROL
DIFFICULTY RATING: 7
TEKKERS RATING: 8
FREQUENTLY USED BY: NEYMAR

Jez: Sometimes you just want to show the ball (and the world) who's boss. Answer: you are. I saw Neymar do this for Barcelona in a game against Real Betis, and the crowd absolutely loved it. Football is about entertainment, as much as it is about winning and – as a Brazilian – Neymar knows this better than most.

The trick for this one is to stand on your weaker leg and bring your stronger leg around the back of your calf. Let the ball strike your instep and remember to keep that foot floppy, so it absorbs the pace of the ball. Magic – it's just like watching Brazil.

WAIT...

...AS THE BALL APPROACHES...

PLACE ONE FOOT BEHIND THE OTHER KNEE

KEEP YOUR FOOT FLOPPY

ABSORB THE FULL WEIGHT OF THE PASS

KILL IT DEAD AND RACE AWAY

TEKKERS MASTERS:
ZINEDINE ZIDANE

'THE DADDY OF MODERN-DAY BALLERS.'

ZINEDINE ZIDANE

SPEED:	6
VISION:	10
TOUCH:	9
FINISHING:	8
TEKKERS:	9

F2 TRUMPS

Billy: Zidane, he's one of Jeremy's favourite players. So he'll be able to tell us more. But I know he was a master on the ball. One of the things about being a pro is protecting the ball, it's about retention. The way he made everything look so easy on the pitch was great.

Jez: OK, now it feels like we've reached the daddy of modern-day ballers. He was such an elegant talent, with such composure. His vision was off the scale, his control was nearly impossibly brilliant. His overall technique would blow you away every time.

Like a lot of us he got the bug early, you know. He learned to play football on the streets of La Castellane in Marseille, France. That's where his skills came from – and his passion. As well as being talented, what stood out was that he wanted the ball all the time. I never once saw him hide.

Billy: That's right. He believed he was the best player on the pitch and went about his game to back this up. It was like he was dancing at times: he'd float along with the ball, then suddenly cut, turn and switch directions. All those step-overs and spins. He was ace at keeping possession too. He kept his head up and his eyes wide open and he shielded the ball well. Want to get the ball off of him? Good luck with that! But he wasn't just some show-off – he was a team-player through and through. He'd make his team-mates look better.

Jez: So let's talk about his goal against Bayer Leverkusen in the UCL final 2002. The assist came from Roberto Carlos – it was a high cross, which would have thrown some players in itself. But you can watch him on the video as it comes in; he's setting himself before the ball even arrives. That's proper composure.

Billy: Fail to prepare and prepare to fail!

Jez: Then the way he takes it with his left foot is sublime. He was already spinning into position before the ball arrived; he knew what was going to happen and what he was going

'WANT TO GET THE BALL OFF OF HIM? GOOD LUCK WITH THAT!'

to do. Then he volleys it exactly where he knows the keeper will have no chance. He's actually continuing the spin as he scores.

Billy: Tekkers! But also look at how much space he'd found himself in. The man had long been considered the best player and yet he'd snuck away from the attention of the Leverkusen defenders and got himself acres of space in the biggest game of the season.

Jez: And now he manages Real. Just think, if he starts passing on his genius… a production line of mini-Zizous being pinged out, one after the other! Dunno if we'll see his like again, though. He won La Liga, Serie A, Champions League, World Cup, European Championship – the lot. Not only that, he defined tournaments and seasons.

Billy: He also took home a ton of personal honours: he was named the FIFA World Player of the Year three times and won the Ballon d'Or. He was named best European soccer player of the past 50 years in the Uefa golden jubilee poll and was included in the FIFA 100, Pelé's list of the 125 greatest living players.

Jez: Imagine being praised by Pelé!

Billy: We don't have to; he described our skills as 'unbelievable', remember?

Jez: I do remember, mate. I was just teeing ya up there!

Billy: And I tucked it away.

Jez: High-five.

PLANET F2

Billy: Without a doubt, travelling the world is one of the privileges of being in The F2. We get to fly around, visiting amazing places, doing the thing we love most.

Jez: I'll always remember the first time I went to New York. It just captured my imagination. I love the skyline, the culture, the energy. The food's not bad either! It's an amazing city.

My favourite place has been Brazil, though. Man, I loved Rio de Janeiro so much! The beach, the vibe – it's all amazing. You know, Brazil is just a footballing nation. It's the heart of the game. Most of my favourite players when I was growing up were Brazilian. And it's every bit as stunning out there as you might imagine: people playing beach soccer. I liked it.

As Bill said, it's such a privilege to be able to travel. It's amazing to be able to travel the world through doing what we're doing. Football is a universal language so there are no barriers. Give us a person and we can have a kickabout with them. It gets quite deep. It's a beautiful thing.

Dubai is an incredible holiday destination. It doesn't have much history or culture. It's man-made. But it's amazing – the food is lovely.

Billy: I agree with Jez that New York is pretty much unbeatable. Amazing culture. I've been there nine times and probably been to Italy about 79 times! It's an amazing thing. There is a sacrifice with all this travel, though. I've spent a whole summer away from my kids, Amelie and Roman and my wife Katie. But that's the only downside.

At the end of the day, we've loved taking our F2 experience all over the world. As we sit down to write this book, we've already been to all these countries. Look at our F2 arrows, all over planet Earth.

Jez: We're taking over, baby!

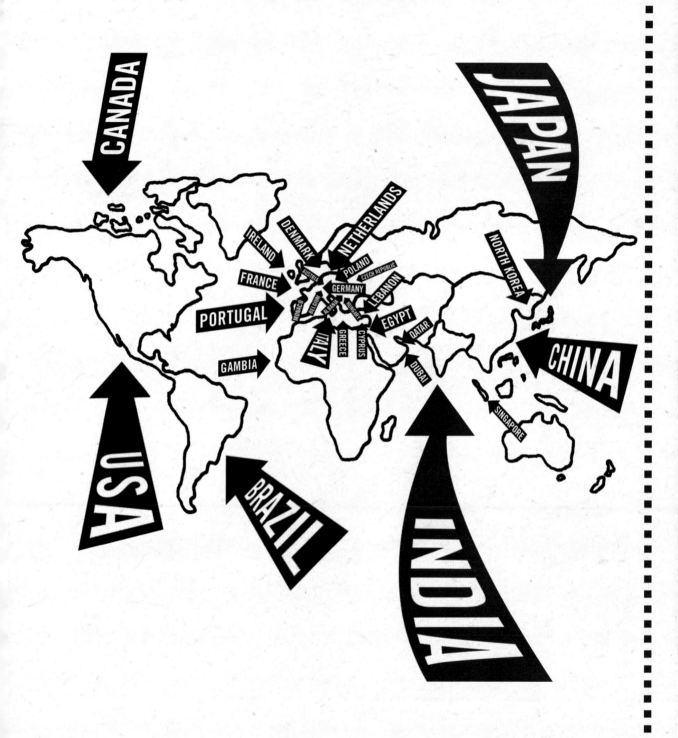

CHAPTER FIVE

THE F2 STORY:
FROM TEKKS TO BECKS

Billy: I read an advert in a careers magazine: 'Do you want to be a schools coach at Arsenal? Fill in this form and freepost it back to us.' I vividly remember completing the form before going to play football at the AstroTurf, as I always did. As I crossed this road, the post box was 500 metres to my left. I stood there, thinking, should I post this or not post this? I could post it or just go straight to football. I stood there trying to decide: do I? Don't I? I eventually thought: I *do*.

Two or three days later they wrote back to me: 'We've applied for you to coach at Arsenal on the youth training scheme (YTS). You're going to be working three days a week on the pitch.' This was a college scheme. They would train me to be a coach on a two-year course. I got the bus from Waltham Cross, just north of the M25, to Holloway in north London, a 90-minute journey – so epic! There were some 36 kids from all over London going for the interview. I was really nervous. All of us were competing for 15 places. I immediately realised I was the only one wearing a suit. Off the back of that I got the scholarship and that's where I learned my trade.

It turned out to be a very useful preparation for the freestyling path. I learned how to be a good coach, how to be around kids, talk to them and be confident in front of them. Being able to engage younger people is really important to us. It helps us make our YouTube videos perfect for them. To be able to think like

'I'D LOOK INSIDE MYSELF FOR GUIDANCE AND MOTIVATION.'

'JUST THINK ABOUT HOW FEW PEOPLE IN THAT STADIUM CAN DO WHAT YOU DO. THERE'S NOT ONE'

kids and enter their world is great, anyway. Their planet is brilliant – no worries on your shoulders, everything's open, everything's free.

Once I had decided to take the freestyling route, I became obsessive. I was really determined to achieve everything I could. I'd go to a local AstroTurf on my own, set myself the challenge of hitting the crossbar from 40 yards out on the half-volley. I wouldn't be able to let it go until I'd done that. I'd be out there, however long it took. I set myself goals. I'd look inside myself for guidance and motivation.

I felt a momentum building that helped my belief that I was doing the right thing. People started to ask me to perform tricks at children's birthday parties. They'd offer me £80 to do it. This was what I had been on for a full 90-minute match. Now I was being offered it for a five-minute show. Definitely! Then the money went up: £100, £150, £200…

That's when I decided to make a freestyling DVD. There weren't many high-profile freestylers at this time. There was only really a Korean guy, Mr Woo. He performed in a T-Mobile advert for Man United at half-time. I felt there was an opportunity for me.

I thought if I were a little kid wanting to get into freestyling I'd need a DVD to teach me the freestyle tricks. So I went out to look for one and found it didn't exist. I taught myself the tricks so I could make that DVD. It was sold across the world. We produced the second one as The F2.

It was that simple. I wanted a DVD. Couldn't find one. So I made one! I was the first. That decision shaped my whole career. I was still playing semi-pro with a team in my spare time. The captain of my football team was a web developer. He worked for

a Japanese TV station as well. I was jogging round, doing a warm-up, on a Thursday night and I approached him: 'Shane, can you build me a website?'

He asked me to explain more, so I told him my vision of the DVD. He said: 'Well, let me have a word with my boss. They invest in projects like this. They're a production team.'

The following week Shane told me a company called Trifield was interested. But they wanted to meet me first. I met a woman called Naomi and we got on really well. To be honest, without the backing of Naomi and Trifield none of this would have been possible. To this day I'm so thankful they believed in me and gave me a platform to start my career off on. They said: 'We'll produce your DVD, fund it and manage you.' So we made the DVD and I did a tour of Japan with it. It was a success. That was where my freestyle career really took off.

Off the back of that, the *Independent* newspaper did a write-up. They were fascinated that someone could make money out of juggling a ball and did a massive article, a double-page spread. Doors were opening one after another. During the interview they'd asked me what my top dream was. I'd said I was a massive Spurs fan and my dream would be to perform on the pitch at White Hart Lane.

As luck would have it, the director of Spurs read that interview on his way into work. That day, they were having a big meeting at the club. They whipped out my article and said: 'What about this guy? What about getting him in as the face of the community side at the club?'

The next thing I knew, I had Spurs on the phone offering me a contract to be their resident freestyler! They said I'd be

expected to do performances at half-time, appear for the club at charity events and give inspirational talks at schools. It was quite an easy 'Yes,' as you can imagine. That took my freestyling to another level and made it my full-time job. I was the first freestyler ever to have a professional contract with a professional football club.

As the stakes rose, so did my nerves. I was so anxious before my first half-time performance at Spurs I said to my dad: 'What if I drop the ball in front of all these Spurs fans?' The more the audience matters the harder it is to get it right. The pressure is more intense. As ever, my wise old dad was on hand to help me out, just as he had when I was a little schoolboy.

He looked me in the eyes and said: 'Just think about how few people in that stadium can do what you do. There's not one.'

He was right. I take that message with me now for all The F2 work. After all, we're only human; we're not robots. The key is to think, in the grand scheme of things, how much does the possibility of a small mistake matter? I prepare as well as I can and I've always thought if I can honestly say I've prepared as well as I can, then I can rest easily. What more can anyone ask?

Talking to kids as part of the Spurs job was a challenge, initially, but I grew to love it. I'd never been a confident guy at school, apart from when it came to playing football. But when I got asked to do coaching and talks as part of my Spurs gig, I was excited about both. In the end it was so motivational to be doing those appearances. I've even done a talk at my daughter, Amelie's school. It's so satisfying to be able to give positive messages.

I think it does have an impact on kids and that means the world to me.

As my freestyling picked up and the Spurs role developed, I started to meet players. Really famous players. I remember the day I met David Beckham. How could I forget? I was freestyling individually when Terry Byrne – David's manager and now our manager too – approached me to ask me to perform at a charity event with Beckham. As I was warming up, Terry said: 'Don't look now but David Beckham's coming.' He literally came over, introduced himself and spent about eight minutes just talking to me, asking me questions about my life. It was presidential!

Honestly, out of all the famous people I've met, David Beckham has the biggest aura. When you're in his presence, you can feel that he's a global superstar. I remember after about four or five minutes of talking, I looked at him and thought:

this is David Beckham! And I suddenly lost the ability to speak for a bit! It was so funny. He's polite, though. For all his success and fame he's still such a humble guy. That must take some doing.

I also met the prime minister! I performed in front of Gordon Brown when he had the top job in the land. Spurs had launched a government project so kids in deprived areas could come and play for free. He came to the launch and I was performing. He said, 'Incredible skills' and shook my hand. I was so excited. The security he came with was off the scale – ten cars with blacked-out windows, police… the works.

As well as meeting pros and stars, I also started to meet other freestylers. There weren't an awful lot of us about at that stage, so we'd keep bumping into one another. One of them always stood out. His name was Jeremy Lynch.

GET THE SKILLS:
RABONA

FACT FILE

ORIGIN: INVENTED BY RICARDO INFANTE 1948, ARGENTINA

SKILL TYPE: SHOT/PASS/CROSS

DIFFICULTY RATING: 6

TEKKERS RATING: 9

FREQUENTLY USED BY: ERIC LAMELA, NEYMAR, DMITRI PAYET, PAUL GASCOIGNE

Billy: This super skill was invented in 1948 by an Argentine baller called Ricardo Infante. Not only did he pull off the first rabona, he scored a goal with it – and that's how you put a new trick on the map.

To nail the rabona you strike the ball by whipping your weaker leg around the back of your standing leg. You can use this to bamboozle an opponent, to avoid using your weaker leg when your positioning isn't ideal, or just to show off.

Follow our step-by-step guide and set your intention to do whatever it takes to master this baby – good luck!

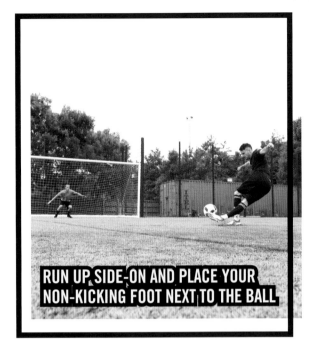

RUN UP SIDE-ON AND PLACE YOUR NON-KICKING FOOT NEXT TO THE BALL

SWING YOUR STRIKING FOOT AROUND THE BACK OF YOUR STANDING LEG

MAKE CONTACT WITH YOUR LACES ON THE UNDERSIDE OF THE BALL

START YOUR RUN UP FROM SIDE-ON

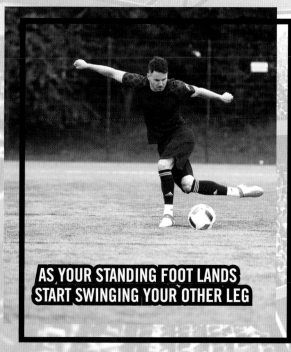

AS YOUR STANDING FOOT LANDS START SWINGING YOUR OTHER LEG

KEEP YOUR STANDING KNEE BENT

FOLLOW-THROUGH UNTIL YOUR KICKING LEG IS STRAIGHT

SWIVEL YOUR HIPS FOR MORE POWER

NEYMAR

'PASSING, SKILLS, SHOOTING, TOUCH, FREESTYLE – YOU NAME IT, HE'S GOT IT.'

Jez: Neymar's such a nice guy. As soon as you meet him you can just tell that he's such a pleasant, genuine person. Not one bit of arrogance. He's overflowing with ability, whether it's passing, skills, shooting, touch, freestyle – you name it, he's got it. He's just got the full package. I believe he will win a Ballon d'Or in the near future. He's the next big thing, believe me. After Messi and Ronaldo, it's Neymar.

Billy: When we made the video with Neymar we had 45 minutes to have a kickaround with him. We shared tekkers. Like Jez says, he's so kind-hearted. A good person.

Jez: He can be quite quiet, though. Maybe he's a little bit shy. But he started to come out of himself at the end of the video. He's just a really nice guy, man. He's up for anything. When you make a suggestion –

NEYMAR

SPEED:	9
VISION:	8
TOUCH:	9
FINISHING:	8
TEKKERS:	10

F2 TRUMPS

even juggling a toilet roll – he's like: 'Yeah, sure, no problem.'

Billy: Just like defenders find it hard to rein in Neymar on the pitch, playing-wise it can be hard to fence him in on the page. He has played in all the attacking positions and tends to roam around the pitch like a pro. He's electric, explosive and excellent.

Jez: All the things beginning with 'e' basically.

Billy: All of them. He's got great pace and playmaking. That doesn't begin with 'e' though.

Jez: What I like about Neymar is that, even as one of the 21st century's greatest talents, he says he is always trying to perfect and improve his game. That shows humility and professionalism. It's also a scary prospect, right? Just think, right now he may only be half as good as he'll become. Who'll be able to stop him then?

Billy: There's not many that can stop him now. Remember that goal he scored against Flamengo a few years back? He beat two defenders by the touchline, took two more opponents out of the game with a simple pass, then ran on to be ready for the return pass. When he got the ball back, he carried on towards the goal, ignoring the defender on his tail, pulled off a quick dummy that took him into the box and then, as two defenders and the keeper zoomed in on him, he had the composure to chip it over the keeper.

'HE'S BEEN COMPARED TO PELÉ. TO PELÉ!.'

Jez: A perfectly timed ending to a ridiculous move. And he was ridiculously good when we met him for the videos. On the crossbar challenge he scored four out of five, but things got really unreal when he did the juggling with random objects. He managed 39 with an orange, 38 with a toilet roll and 25 with football socks.

The kickaround was incredible, too. And what a cool guy all round. Let's look at his skills. One of my favourites is the rocket.

Billy: He steps beside the ball with his strong foot, traps it and lifts off with the same foot. He uses the front of his weaker foot and the heel of his stronger foot. It's massively effective and well worth practising for any footballer, pro or otherwise. He's done that so many times and it always gets the fans off their seats.

I'm also all about the Wingrove-Cruyff. We taught Neymar this, but he's yet to use it in a game! He touches the ball with the outside of his foot, brings his other foot behind and around the ball, swings his leg around his standing foot, touches the ball with the inside of his foot and speeds off.

Jez: When you listen to people who have worked with Neymar, the same word keeps cropping up over and over: genius. Look at his hat-trick against Inter. To score one of those goals he ran at 31 kilometres an hour with the ball stuck to his right boot. Over 65 metres he left five Inter players stranded. He's been compared to Pelé. To Pelé! Ronaldinho and Ronaldo both think he'll become the best player in the world. Decent prospects, hey?

Billy: He's exemplary – another word beginning with an 'e'!

Jez: …

THE F2 HALL OF FAME

ONE OF THE BEST THINGS ABOUT BEING IN THE F2 IS GETTING TO HANG OUT WITH SOME OF THE SUPERSTARS OF THE GAME. HERE'S OUR LIST SO FAR. YOU COULD MAKE A PRETTY DECENT SQUAD FROM THIS LOT!

CHAPTER SIX

THE F2 STORY:

IN SEARCH OF
MARADONA

Jez: It was crazy, as I was surrounded by thousands of talented people, to have the confidence that I could be the best. But that was me when I was young! My mind-set was always that if I was going to do something I was going to do it and be the best. As it turned out I was indeed one of the best ones there. I was popular. Again, it was just about seeing something that hadn't been done before. There had never been a football freestyler on *BGT*. I was full of confidence – I had so much self-belief. I knew I was good. Right from the start, I had a cheekiness that Simon Cowell spotted and seemed to like.

I got through the first early stages. I breezed through to be honest. Got to the judges' stage and smashed it. They said I was the best act they'd seen in London that year and they tipped me to win it outright.

But during the live show I bit off more than I could chew. I needed the voice of experience in my ear, someone to say: 'Jez, you can go at 60 per cent and breeeeze into the final. And you can go at 70 per cent in the final and probably win it.' But I didn't have that assistance so I went for it and tried to do a 100 per cent job. I made a couple of mistakes and was voted out.

I was absolutely devastated. The judges loved me. Amanda said she really liked me. Simon loved me, he said he loved the cheekiness. He said he saw himself in me, in my confidence and my absolutely unshakeable self-belief. I wasn't sure about Piers. But as soon as I started making mistakes they didn't understand. Working with a ball there is always a chance you can get it wrong,

'EVEN MESSI AND RONALDO WILL HAVE HAD TIMES WHEN THEY WERE KNOCKED BACK.'

even if you only kick the ball a millimetre off. So they felt they had no choice but to tell me it was the end of my journey. Once again, I was being told I'd done well but it was over. At the time I felt it was the worst thing. It felt as bad as Arsenal. I felt public humiliation. I'm a perfectionist and I was not pleased with my performance or myself.

But you know what? People still come up to me and say: 'Jez, we remember you on *BGT*!' This showed me that car-crash TV can actually work – people are sometimes more likely to remember the ones who crashed and burned than the ones who did well. When I stood in front of them I was not at all phased. I was full of confidence. I think that came across. Simon said to me: 'I can see that you've definitely got star quality.' And that has since developed

even further. Simon was warm to me backstage. I noticed he singled me out and was more friendly with me than most of the other contestants. He really took a shine to me. It's crazy how he can see potential quicker than most.

I take positives where I can. Knockdowns and setbacks will happen. Even Messi and Ronaldo will have had times when they were knocked back.

Next up, I was asked to appear in a film called *In the Hands of the Gods*. It was to be the true story of five young British freestyle footballers' journey across the Americas to Argentina in the hope of meeting their hero, Diego Maradona. The idea was we had to raise the money to get there by busking our skills in the street and by blagging our travel and accommodation along the

'I'M PROUD THAT I STAYED TRUE TO MY BELIEFS.'

way. The film had a proper load of talent behind it, including both Ben Winston, who'd worked with One Direction, Manchester United and James Corden as well as Gabe Turner, who had done stuff with Usain Bolt.

It was great. I was on a five-week mission to meet Diego Maradona. This was at a time when he was really elusive. So people were wondering where he was, what he was up to. Since then he's been more visible in public, doing a bit of management and so on. He's out there. But back then, nobody really knew what he was up to.

So it was a brilliant concept and became a great film. The key moment came when we had only raised enough money for two flights from the US to Argentina. We had to decide what to do. I stayed true to my values, which are very much based on loyalty. I felt we should have stayed together as a group of five, but there was a divide when some wanted to go their own way. That was when we had a disagreement. To this day I stick by what I felt at the time: you should be loyal to your friends, just as you should to your family. Stick together and live or die as a team.

I didn't get to meet Maradona, others did. But, overall, making the film was a memorable experience. I took a lot from it. I learned what makes a good film, whether it's a movie or a YouTube video. A plot twist doesn't do a movie any harm. Looking back, that disagreement and the vote we took made for great footage; great content. I understand that now. But I'm proud that I stayed true to my beliefs. And, let's be honest, if we had stayed

together, would all of us have made it? I don't know. But for me, when you start something as a team, you finish it as a team. I firmly believe that.

The film went into cinemas. It did really well and went on to be one of the most successful British docu-films of all time. All of this helped to build my confidence, when I hadn't always been so self-assured. Back then, it was a learning curve. Being able to freestyle also helped. Having to perform. What I learned quickly was that I shouldn't transfer a negative mood to my audience. Whatever it seems to those watching that I'm feeling as a performer will be shared by them. So I learned to project confidence. It became an everyday thing for me and I became quite different to the shy kid I had been.

Off the back of the exposure I got

from *BGT*, I launched my first YouTube video. This was pre-The F2 and was just me on my own doing skills. I did the video because I wanted it to come out in sync with the film. I imagined that people watching the film would be thinking, 'Who's that Jeremy Lynch kid?' When they typed my name into Google, I wanted an amazing video to come up. I've no idea if this is what happened, but the video did end up going viral, which makes it seem like it was all part of the plan.

I filmed the video on a camcorder. I got my cousin to piece it together, because I didn't know how to edit. It has racked up millions and millions of views. It was the first time I had got my name out there on the internet. Soon, I was on the circuit and I bumped into a guy who would change my life beyond recognition.

GET THE SKILLS:
WINGROVE CRUYFF

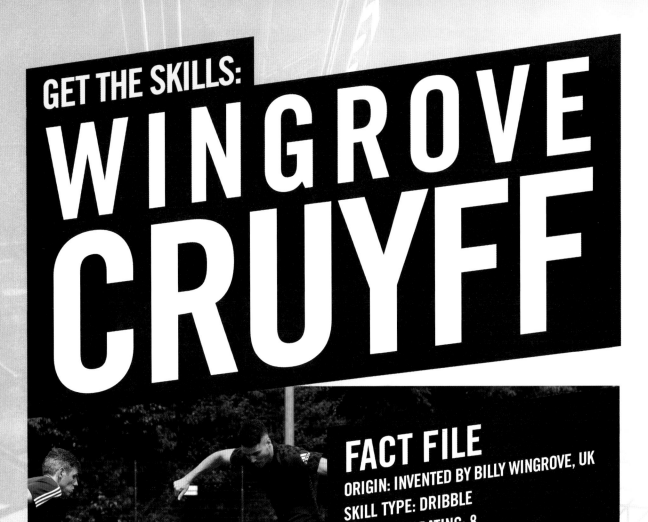

FACT FILE
ORIGIN: INVENTED BY BILLY WINGROVE, UK
SKILL TYPE: DRIBBLE
DIFFICULTY RATING: 8
TEKKERS RATING: 9
FREQUENTLY USED BY: MR B. WINGROVE

Billy: Imagine this: a potent cocktail of the best of me and the best of Dutch football uber-legend Johan Cruyff. Cruyff was famous for leaving defenders marking fresh air. His brain was as quick as his feet too. No wonder he's idolised by Pep Guardiola.

The Dutch are known for honing their skills by taking 10,000 touches of a football a day. And this one's going to take a bit of practice: the key thing is to follow the steps closely, and then build up the speed slowly. But, anything Jo-han do, you can do better… (sorry).

TOUCH THE BALL WITH THE INSIDE OF YOUR BOOT

THEN THE OUTSIDE...

... CUTTING SLIGHTLY BACKWARDS

CROSS YOUR STANDING LEG BEHIND THE BALL...

...BUT SO THAT IT LANDS IN FRONT OF THE BALL

NOW TAP THE BALL FORWARDS USING YOUR INSTEP BEHIND YOUR LEG

...AND RACE AWAY

EDEN HAZARD

'HOW MANY TIMES HAVE WE SEEN HIM MAKE A FOOL OUT OF DEFENDERS?'

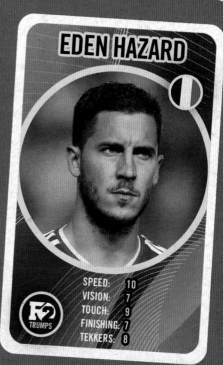

EDEN HAZARD

SPEED:	10
VISION:	7
TOUCH:	9
FINISHING:	7
TEKKERS:	8

F2 TRUMPS

Billy: Eden Hazard is yet another superstar that it was a complete joy to work with. He's a really small guy, with incredibly quick feet. We did a challenge with him in which he had to rabona the ball onto the bar. Most players would take a couple of goes, but him? He did it first time. That, for me, sums him up. His talent is incredible and he's proved it time and time again. I think he's only going to get better. I don't think we've seen the best of him yet, I really don't.

Jez: If you want a baller who has got everything, Eden Hazard has got to be on your list. He's got blinding pace, unbelievable balance and stunning creative power. He's composed and adaptable in the tightest of situations.

Billy: So adaptable. He's played out wide, as an attacking midfielder, a number ten – the works. When Diego Costa was out they moved him even further forward and he made a difference. He also responds to his gaffer. When Mourinho told him he had to work a bit harder and track back more, he did just that. No sulks, just a professional response and it made him so much more of a player.

Jez: Yeah, he's become a stronger and stronger athlete. He can ride tackles and bounces back quickly when he's kicked. Flair players are not always as hardy as that. He's also got unreal desire and hunger, it's like he's never satisfied. And those lungs – it's like he's got the capacity of a bull. So you're right, he's got all you'd want from a player.

Billy: His passing, though…

Jez: Yes, he can spray that ball around with so much accuracy. That's why he gets so many

assists, he can make the ball do just what he wants it to. It's actually stunning. I love watching him play!

Billy: What about when we met up with him for our video? Talk about training with the maestro! You had to do some push-up punishment when you broke down the chain.

Jez: Thanks for reminding me. What are you chatting about, anyway? He gave you a yellow card!

Billy: Ha! Fair play. His crossbar shot was something else, though. And the way he just walked off with his back to it. Didn't even hang around to see if he'd managed it. He knew he had!

Jez: He says that even as a kid he was obsessed with tricks and flicks. At six he was doing keepy-uppies for hours, he was also mastering nutmegs and copying Maradona's roulette trick. It all pays off; how many times have we seen him make a fool out of defenders? He roams past them and they just end up sliding along for miles.

Billy: Resistance is futile! It shows again that hard work pays off. All that practice he started so young had results. Remember his double nutmeg against Southampton? Boom, boom! See ya later!

Jez: And people say he should work on his finishing to become a proper great but from where I'm sitting his finishing is awesome. Remember his solo goal against Liverpool? It was magnificent – I loved the way he took his time in the build-up. He didn't just run wildly at goal and risk losing the ball. He went backwards, forwards, even sideways – whatever it took to keep possession. When the time was right, he just simply mazed his way into the area and scored.

Billy: You know, even the way he takes penalties is a class apart. Next time you see him step up, watch his body language. He gives nothing away and the keeper can't tell which way he's going to go with the spot kick. He's been compared to Messi and Ronaldo. It doesn't get much better than that.

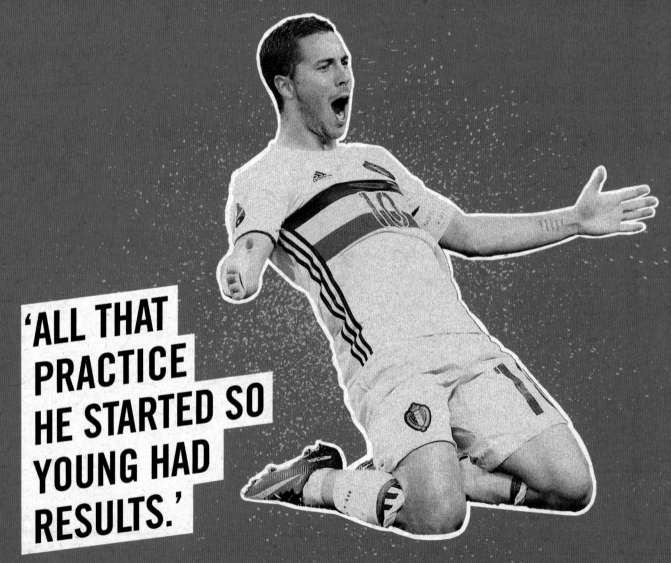

'ALL THAT PRACTICE HE STARTED SO YOUNG HAD RESULTS.'

BUILD
YOUR OWN
DREAM TEAM

(AND SEND IT TO OUR TWITTER @F2FREESTYLERS WITH THE HASHTAG #F2FC)

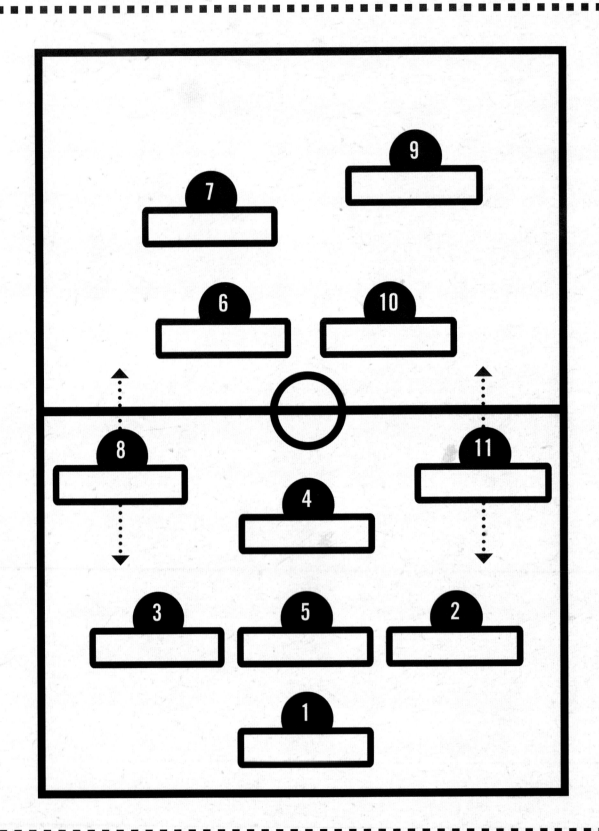

CHAPTER SEVEN

THE F2 STORY:
ORIGINS: THE F2

Billy: I actually remember when I first met Jez, at a football tournament in Redbridge. Someone had tried to start a troupe of freestylers called… The Freestylers.

Jez: Genius name. How did they come up with that?

Billy: Ha, ha! To be fair, the idea never went far. We turned up and Jez was there with a company doing some freestyling. I looked over at him and thought: Wow, he's really good. I introduced myself and we hit it off quickly. He came over and joined The Freestylers.

He was so quiet back then – extremely so at times. He's Christian, he went to a private school and he hadn't had much contact with the outside world. He really hadn't. He was really vulnerable as a kid, was Jez.

Jez: It's true. Because I used to be quite shy, you know? You wouldn't believe it now, but I was quite introverted, back in the day.

Billy: But he soon started to emerge from his shell. We did our first job together for a construction company. It was at an exhibition in Birmingham. There were five of us. Me and Jez got on particularly well. We became really good friends. We started to take more odd jobs here and there together. I had an agent; Jez had come out of *Britain's Got Talent* but didn't have an agent, so he had enthusiasm but not necessarily the direction.

I told him to come on board with my agent and he did. We kept working together. We parted ways with our agent and decided to create a double act. There was a sense that this was year zero in a way, because we had individual profiles: me at Spurs, Jez fresh from *BGT*. We had to sacrifice those individual standings and put everything into the partnership. It was exciting for us to become a two-piece act.

'JEZ WAS THERE DOING SOME FREESTYLING. I LOOKED OVER AT HIM AND THOUGHT: WOW, HE'S REALLY GOOD.'

All the time, more people were joining the community looking to make a successful career from freestyle. And more top brands were looking to hire freestylers. It was a surging thing. Therefore, the competition was going up, too. At the end of the day, though, any new talented face is good for freestyle. It ups the bar, which means we all have to raise our game.

Jez: Yeah, we both had a profile before but we moved away from our individual identities and branded everything as The F2. A new logo, a new combined identity. It was a big decision, because Billy already had 5,000 followers on his own YouTube account. To lose those and go for a new combined following was brave. Now we've got over 4 million followers, so it was the right decision!

We also both agreed that we would commit all our time and energy to The F2. We would commit our lives to it. We both believed in it and knew it had massive potential. Thankfully, it's gone even better than we imagined – and we imagined it would be big!

Billy: Who knows if we would have become as big in mainstream football as we have in what we do now. I think Jez could have.

Jez: I feel like Bill sells himself a bit short sometimes. I think he could have done a lot more in the game than he thinks. But all the opportunities we were getting meant we had to stay sharp on the tricks and commit to it. We couldn't do both. Nobody now could say how successful we could have been in football had we channelled all our energies into that. Even we couldn't guess. But I would like to do a documentary with us dipping back into the game. It would be very interesting to see what level we could make it to. I believe we could take it to a very high standard. I like to believe that, anyway!

'WE ALSO BOTH AGREED THAT WE WOULD COMMIT ALL OUR TIME AND ENERGY TO THE F2. WE WOULD COMMIT OUR LIVES TO IT.'

Billy: It has worked out. What we are doing has never been done before in the history of mankind! Who could have predicted how quickly social media would take over the world?

We never compete, we're always together. We share everything. We each want the other to be the best they can be.

Jez: What I do remember is that we got on very well from the off. We had no idea we were about to create one of the biggest social media football superpowers, but there was so much chemistry from the start. We'd keep bumping into each other, because there weren't that many people doing it back then.

Billy: We're the perfect combination because we're so different. Jez is very creative, he plays piano, he's really laid-back, relaxed, chilled out, calm. If we were the same people, we'd probably argue. But we never argue. I honestly don't think there's any partnership in work that goes as well as me and Jez.

Jez: It's true.

Billy: He's a very witty guy, too. He makes me laugh a lot. He's really funny. Great banter. He can banter anyone, Jez can. That's important when you're filming, it makes it so much easier.

Jez: Thanks, man. I don't think I'm the funniest guy in the world but I do think I've got an understanding of comedic timing. On camera I clown around a lot but I'm a serious person, too. I've got my head

screwed on tight, my feet on the ground. I'm intelligent and strategic. That's one aspect of me. Then there's the clowning part of me. I'm both of those people. I know how to make a video funny, whether it's through being funny during the filming or editing it to make it even funnier.

Billy: It's true. His stuff off-camera is also as funny or sometimes funnier than on-camera. I'll laugh all the way home, sometimes. I'll text him and tell him how much he made me crack up. Sometimes it will just be a look he gives me at a particular moment.

Jez: Freestyle has evolved. We were in the first wave, we were the pioneers. But there is a difference: a lot of the freestylers today started by doing freestyle. They wanted to

do it from a young age, started practising as kids and that's all they ever wanted to do. Whereas me and Billy, our foundation has always been football. We wanted to be footballers as children, we played for football teams in academies and maintained a high level of fitness. Doing tricks was like a branching off from football for us. Then we made a career from the tricks.

The market has got over-saturated and it did reach a point where the whole thing had kind of been seen. It wasn't brand-new any more. It became almost impossible to impress people, to get that same reaction from audiences as when it all started.

So, for us, we were two of the first to see that the novelty had died away. What can we do next, to stay at the top of our game and stay fresh and entertaining? How can we keep that wow factor?

RONALDO KNUCKLEBALL

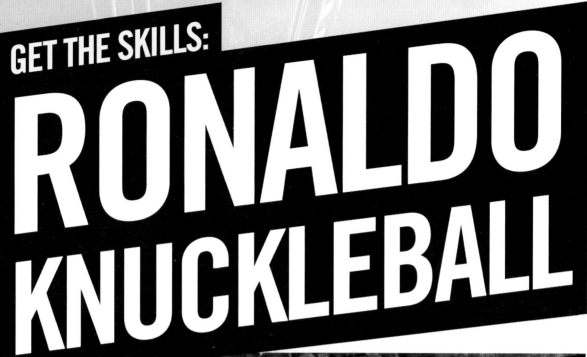

FACT FILE

ORIGIN: CAN BE TRACED BACK TO BASEBALL, EARLY 1900s

SKILL TYPE: SHOT

DIFFICULTY RATING: 10

TEKKERS RATING: 10

FREQUENTLY USED BY: CRISTIANO RONALDO, JUNINHO PERNAMBUCANO, GARETH BALE

Jez: I love a knuckleball, you love a knuckleball, everybody loves a knuckleball. We're going to show you how to hit the trademark free kick that the likes of Cristiano Ronaldo and Gareth Bale have perfected.

The aim of this strike is to get the ball moving in the air. You don't need to hit it hard, but you do need to hit it right. Once you've followed these simple steps, then it's all about practice, practice, practice. It can take time to reach perfection. But, then you'll be unstoppable.

Now I think about, there are people who don't like knuckleballs – goalkeepers.

APPROACH THE BALL ON YOUR TOES AT A 45 DEGREE ANGLE

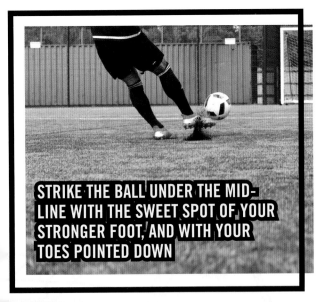

STRIKE THE BALL UNDER THE MID-LINE WITH THE SWEET SPOT OF YOUR STRONGER FOOT, AND WITH YOUR TOES POINTED DOWN

STOP YOUR FOOT AFTER STRIKING THE BALL — THERE'S NO NEED TO FOLLOW THROUGH

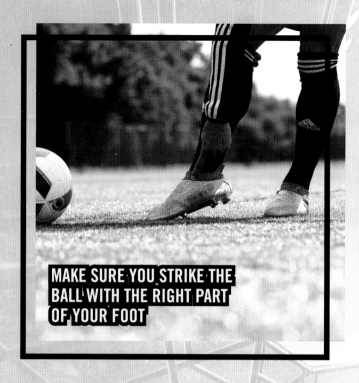

MAKE SURE YOU STRIKE THE BALL WITH THE RIGHT PART OF YOUR FOOT

LEAN FORWARD WHEN RUNNING UP TO THE BALL

THE PERFECT KNUCKLEBALL SHOULD HAVE NO SPIN AT ALL!

THE PERFECT KNUCKLEBALL...

...IS UNSAVEABLE

131

STEVEN GERRARD

'VERY FEW PLAYERS IN THE HISTORY OF THE GAME HAVE A SWEETER STRIKE THAN STEVIE G.'

STEVEN GERRARD

SPEED: 8
VISION: 9
TOUCH: 7
FINISHING: 10
TEKKERS: 7

F2 TRUMPS

Jez: This man has got the sweetest strike of any player we've ever worked with. He's also a great guy, really humble. Think of all he's achieved and yet he's a hundred per cent down to earth. We got on really well and we've met up a few times since. We've become mates. He's specifically asked to make more videos with us because he enjoyed it so much.

That was a great day. We were whacking in shots for three-quarters of an hour. One of my favourite experiences throughout The F2. The power and swaz he gets on his shots is almost unbelievable to see in person. Very few players in the history of the game have a sweeter strike than Stevie G. He didn't disappoint, he was absolutely fantastic.

Billy: I totally agree. If you're looking for a man who defined a club and who was defined by a club, then you won't find a better example than Steven Gerrard. He joined Liverpool aged nine and never played for another UK club; he stuck with the Reds. He was Mr Liverpool.

Jez: Not that he was short of offers. I mean, how many times did José Mourinho try to get him to Chelsea?

Billy: Loads. No wonder, either. What a player he was. He had pace, stamina and a proper work ethic. But he was about more than the slog: his vision, touch, and his precise passing range were amazing. And he could just burn past defenders. They'd slide in to him but he'd just say: 'See ya later, pal!' Not to mention that he had quite a shot on him. How many times did he score from miles out?

Jez: He always seemed to be arriving just at the right moment to lash it home. That timing is a form of genius, you know? He was also better in the air than he's sometimes given credit for. When I think back to Gerrard I remember him as a

'HE WAS MR LIVERPOOL.'

ridiculously good box-to-box midfielder, but he also played so many other positions in his time: a holding midfielder, attacking midfielder, a right-back, and a right-winger. He even ran out as a second striker sometimes!

Billy: He seemed to just take over games, didn't he? He sparked the fight-back in the 2005 Champions League final. He led the way as they came back from three goals down against AC Milan. They were dead and buried at half-time! But then he scored a goal and won a pen; next thing you know – boom, Liverpool are on the flight home with the trophy.

Jez: My favourite game of all time. I also remember him beating Olympiakos more-or-less single-handedly, his two goals against Real Madrid and his hat-trick in a Merseyside derby. A big game player with a massive heart.

Billy: He must have a pretty big sideboard, too. He won everything there is apart from the Premier League – the Uefa Cup, FA cups, League cups – and England caps, of course.

Jez: Your favourite Gerrard goal?

Billy: Maybe his volley against West Ham in the FA Cup final. That was special. He must have been more than 30 yards out. And he did the same trick against so many teams, including Manchester United. He left Barthez stranded. Those two goals alone show that his best moments came when it really counted.

Jez: Nice. An absolute icon and a man we cannot wait to work with again.

DESIGN YOUR OWN BOOT

(AND SEE IT COME ALIVE)

137

CHAPTER EIGHT

THE F2 STORY:
NEXT LEVEL: THE F2

Jez: Billy came up with the idea of creating a double act because there had never been a freestyle double act before. We would be the first. So we did it. That was our niche. We thought: OK, so that's our niche, that's great. But is there anything more we can do to make it even more our thing? So we had the idea to do the performances in suits. It was very commercial, because freestyle hadn't been done that way. Freestyle was seen as a very urban thing with a brick wall and graffiti. That was like the go-to environment for freestyle – very urban. We thought we'd appeal to businesses, to gala dinners and award ceremonies. We spent months working on a master double-act routine. Our unspoken motto would be: everything with excellence. We still make sure we follow that.

Within a year we got invited to open the Ballon d'Or ceremony. It was the most surreal, intense and high-pressure experience we've had. And it went really, really well. From Messi to Ronaldo, from Mourinho to Guardiola, the audience was properly star-studded. Anyone who was anyone in football was there – all eyes on us. All we had was two footballs and suits. We smashed the show. No mistakes, no drops, neat and tidy, all in sync. We got an incredible reaction. Afterwards, Cristiano Ronaldo sought us out to tell us how impressed he was and how pleased.

We got a lot of bookings after that. We were the undisputed freestyling double act! Again, we thought: how can we take this to the next level? So we started the YouTube channel. We saw that social media was at the very beginning of something new. YouTube was something new, Instagram and Snapchat weren't invented, Facebook was something different to what it is now. It was just a way for friends and family to stay in touch and up to date with one another. Even Twitter was relatively new. But we knew that social media was going to get bigger and bigger. As with everything, we had to be proactive rather than reactive.

'OUR UNSPOKEN MOTTO WOULD BE: EVERYTHING WITH EXCELLENCE.'

We had to be ahead of the game. We started up accounts across all networks and began making videos. Instantly, we realised we could make really good videos. It wasn't long before we realised that there was more to it than stage shows. As soon as that penny dropped we started making more videos, putting more time into them, uploading consistently, keeping the quality high. We've never looked back.

Our following was picking up steadily over about three years before it just rocketed. It's like we turned a corner and it showed we'd made the right decision when we combined all our networks and contacts and followers.

Billy: I think with The F2 and our careers, we've always tried to stay on top of the game and progress. Like we said, we started out as individual performers and, once we felt like that had been seen and done, we noticed that it was all about individuals. Nobody had done

'WE WERE THE UNDISPUTED FREESTYLING DOUBLE ACT!'

a double act. We won Event Awards' UK Entertainment Act of the Year award in 2012 and saw there were some YouTubers who were putting their skills online and teaching young kids. We wanted to go down that route and see what we could make of it. Football on YouTube wasn't such a thing back then, there was only, like, one football channel that we knew about at the time.

We had the skills, we had the talent, and with YouTube it's amazing – you can put one video out and anyone across the world can see it. You hit so many people and really impact them. Off the back of that award we thought: 'Right, YouTube is the next step.' We wanted to progress from performing individually, to performing as a double act and then YouTube.

We didn't think for one moment it would get as big as it's got now.

Jez: In the run-up to winning that Event Awards' trophy, we studied some of our

favourite entertainers, across all genres, because we knew we had the football techniques but we wanted to work on the entertainment dimension of our act. In a nutshell, we studied Michael Jackson, Diversity and a masked American dance group called the Jabbawockeez. We created a routine that combined the best of those three acts with our football tricks. Within a year it was doing well and bookings were flying in. That was when we were nominated for UK Entertainment Act of the Year and won it. So we had a title! Then we moved into YouTube.

Billy: And we soon found out how obsessive you can become about YouTube. I got obsessed with the stats and the data. Every morning, one of the first things I do is get on Social Blade, a website that measures social media stats, and check: how many views we've got and all the demographics. With every video, we start monitoring 20 minutes after it goes live. We know where we expect it to be after 20 minutes, then after one hour, two hours, three hours, and overnight. I have become obsessed with it all: how many 'likes' we've got, what people are saying in the comments and so on.

We've got quite a wide variety of videos. Some of it is trial and error. So we use all this to shape what we film and how we film. Meta tags, keywords, all of that determines how many views we get. Just putting in the right words and phrases can add as many as 5 million views to one video. I leave a lot of the video work to Jez. I manage the Rascal Clothing side of things and he runs the YouTube side of things.

We both love it. It's so easy to post whatever content we like and to engage with people all over the world. It's so great – we go out and film the videos, have fun, then Jeremy edits the videos and we post them. And they're there forever! When we've retired and grown old, our kids and our kids' kids – they'll always be able to see what we achieved. It's like leaving behind a legacy. A great legacy, in fact.

Billy: Jez, do you remember when we put our first video up?

Jez: Yeah, I do. I hadn't been trained in editing but I got the hang of it quite quickly. The first video I edited was Billy's. He asked me if I could work on his wedding video. I bought an editing programme and gave it a real push. I was pleased with the result – it was certainly the best wedding video I'd ever seen! I realised I could do this. So I couldn't wait for us to put our first video online.

I believe that the fact I edit has been a key part of The F2. I think I have become at least as good at the editing as I am the tekkers. Maybe better. I've been offered editing gigs but why would I take them and give up The F2?

So, that made our partnership even stronger. It's an unstoppable combination. We've got all the tools that we need. Too many cooks spoil the broth and we both understand that it's better if one of us focuses on one aspect, so we're not treading on one another's toes. But we do consult each other. How it works is on the little decisions, we can make them on our own. On the big decisions, we consult the other one.

GET THE SKILLS:
BACK SNAP

FACT FILE

ORIGIN: NEW EXCLUSIVE SKILL!
INVENTED BY BILLY WINGROVE, UK
SKILL TYPE: PASS
DIFFICULTY RATING: 8
TEKKERS RATING: 10
FREQUENTLY USED BY: MR B. WINGROVE

Billy: This right here is an F2 exclusive. You won't find this skill anywhere else. I call it the back snap. It's not one you're likely to see in a game, but it's going to get you some big love from your team-mates in training.

Simply flick the ball up, turn your back while standing on one leg and bending the other. Then as the ball comes down on the back of your knee extend the bent leg quickly with a snapping movement and watch the ball ping off towards your team-mate.

Actually – I dare you to use it in a game. Just imagine that!

FLICK THE BALL UP

TURN YOUR BACK ON THE BALL AND YOUR TEAM-MATE

LIFT YOUR LEG AND BEND YOUR KNEE...

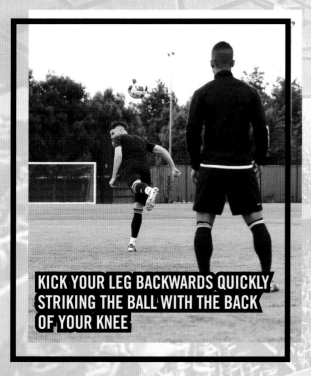

KICK YOUR LEG BACKWARDS QUICKLY STRIKING THE BALL WITH THE BACK OF YOUR KNEE

WATCH IT PING TO YOUR TEAM-MATE

BEND...

SNAP...

PING!

GARETH BALE

'IT'S ONLY WHEN YOU MEET HIM UP CLOSE THAT YOU REALISE WHAT A UNIT HE IS!'

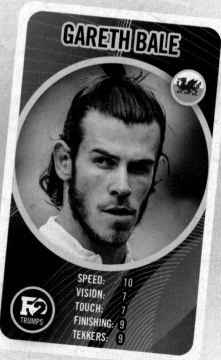

GARETH BALE

SPEED: 10
VISION: 7
TOUCH: 7
FINISHING: 9
TEKKERS: 9

F2 TRUMPS

Jez: Look, the first thing that stands out about this dude is his physique. It's only when you meet him up close that you realise what a unit he is! He's tall; he's not got even an ounce of fat on him. Just like your perfect athlete, really.

He was brilliant with us. The first thing he said was: 'Lads, I don't really do tricks.' But he came across really well. I think he even surprised himself with some of the things he was coming out with. Once he got it, he was trying all sorts of skills. No one has ever seen him in that light. It was a privilege that we got to be the ones to present him to the world in a way that nobody has ever seen.

Billy: Some players have quick legs, other players have quick minds. What Gareth Bale proves once and for all is that if you have both, you're deadly. He's almost unplayable on his day. How would you stop him, readers?

Jez: It's true: defenders are terrified of pace wherever it's situated. And Bale scares the life out of opponents. He goes right at defenders, doesn't he? He lets them get close and then burns past them.

Billy: He's always been in a hurry – he made his international debut at 16. But it really started for him at Spurs….

Jez: Erm, excuse me! I think Southampton might have something to say about that!

Billy: OK, OK! I admit, he started at the Saints and they deserve maximum credit for spotting him as a kid and slotting him right in their team. Sure. But look at how things took off for him at White Hart Lane. We moved him forwards up the pitch and he played in a ton of different positions from

'YOU CAN SEE HOW STRONG HE IS IN HIS HEAD, TOO. HE DOESN'T LET THE PRESSURE DERAIL HIM.'

defence to attack. His game developed big-time. Unbelievable.

Jez: When we met him to do the Adidas X test video it was such a privilege. We did those synchronised moves – talk about pressure on us! When he was doing the keepy-uppies he left us all stunned. I thought it was never going to end – what a juggler! So... your favourite Bale moment for Spurs?

Billy: Probably his Champions League hat-trick against Inter Milan in 2010. If a team's 4-0 down at half-time at the San Siro, how many players might drop their heads? He didn't. He got a second-half hat-trick. People always chat about the first leg, but that's not even half the story. In the second leg he made Inter's right-back, Maicon, look ordinary and make no mistake, Maicon is class.

Jez: Bale's an asset for a team in so many ways. Even in La Liga he's sometimes double-marked. Teams are that scared of him. And that opens up the play for his team-mates, who have that bit more room after Gareth's dragged an extra defender

away or just powered past them. He always seems to have that extra gear and he can change up effortlessly. It's insane to watch!

Billy: The long-range goals he spanks in are crazy; his curling drives, his free kicks. Or when he shoots to the byline and slams a cross in. He's got a packed locker. He even looks like some sort of master species. He's top-notch athletic and properly powerful at the same time. You can see how strong he is in his head, too. When he waits to take a free kick he's so poised and focused. He doesn't let the pressure derail him.

Jez: True words. Micah Richards said Bale 'made me feel an inch tall'. Harry Redknapp said Bale is up there with Messi and Ronaldo and he's won top trophies in Spain. Proper reward for a lifetime of dedication. How cool is it that one of the very best players on the planet comes from Britain?

Billy: And that he honed his trade at the mighty Tottenham?

Jez: All right, Bill, any excuse to mention Spurs.

TOP SECRET

UNTOLD STORIES

YOU'VE WATCHED THE VIDEOS OF US HANGING OUT WITH SO MANY STARS OF THE FOOTBALL GALAXY. BUT WHAT HAPPENED WHEN THE CAMERAS WEREN'T ROLLING? FIND OUT HERE, AS WE TAKE YOU BEHIND THE SCENES TO TELL YOU SOME UNTOLD STORIES...

GARETH BALE

Billy: Pay attention at the back, because I'm about to lay down a fat slice of F2 trivia. Guess who was the first person to meet Gareth Bale after he signed for Spurs from Southampton?

Jez: Oooh... I give up.

Billy: You don't want a clue?

Jez: Bill, you know I already know the answer. Can't we just crack on?

Billy: All right, it was me! Gareth and me were both invited to open a school in North London on his first day of being a Spurs player. So, as a little bit of Tottenham history was made, there I was. Right in there among it all.

Jez: Pretty cool. And something like six or seven years later we filmed with Gareth as The F2. We weren't sure he'd remember Bill. By now he was a big Real Madrid star and so much had happened during those years. But he did remember! He instantly recognised Bill, and came up to him on set straight away.

Billy: We ended up having a right old chat about it all. We spoke about where it first started and what had happened since. Amazing. What a nice guy.

Jez: It's astounding how far you've both come. Gotta hand it to you both.

DIEGO MARADONA

Jez: And now here's the story of a player I almost met. As you know, before The F2, I was involved in a film called *In The Hands of the Gods*. This film had originally been titled *In Search of Diego*. It followed me and four other English freestyle footballers as we tried to raise money by showcasing our skills, all in order to fund a trip to Buenos Aires to meet Diego Maradona.

Billy: If you haven't seen the film then I recommend you seek it out. It's a gripping thing to watch. With no money for food, accommodation or travel, Jez and the others hustle and busk their way from London to Buenos Aires using only their football skills and their charm. They are often forced to go hungry and to sleep rough.

Jez: Yeah. It was tough at times. It was real. Look, there were a lot of twists and turns along the way that resulted in two of the freestylers not meeting Diego.

Billy: And get the violins ready, because poor Jez was one of the two that missed out.

Jez: Gutted. But who would have thought that through The F2 I would get to meet even more top pros and legends – it's amazing really.

LIONEL MESSI

Billy: As you've read and probably seen, we have filmed with Messi, but did you know one of us has been Messi?

Jez: This section is in danger of turning into a quiz show.

Billy: Is that your final answer? Seriously, though, I have body-doubled for the great man in a number of TV commercials. And Jez is just getting testy because he's jealous.

Jez: Ha! Well, it is a pretty cool addition on the old CV, I guess!

Billy: The ads were for Pepsi, PES and a Turkish airlines advert. On that airlines one it includes 'Messi' – that'll be me - and Kobe Bryant on a plane doing skills and tricks. And right here we want to reach out to Messi and say that if he ever wants to body double for me, then he's more than welcome.

Jez: All right, Bill, you're getting carried away there. I think you've done pretty well and it's time for a rest.

DAVID VILLA

Jez: When we work with the top pros we see how much love and passion they have for football. It's just a pure love – and there's no better example of that than David Villa.

Billy: When we filmed with David and Andrea Pirlo in the summer of 2016, we found them both just unbelievable technically. Seriously, they were off the scale of tekkers. It was just so much fun to watch them playing around. Unbelievable privilege.

Jez: Remember when we were filming free kicks with them? They just got into it so much. Particularly David. I remember he had to be literally pulled off the pitch by his management! He'd already trained with the team that morning and he had other commitments later in the day. So they wanted him to stop.

Billy: But it was just beautiful to see his love and passion for the game. Even just having a ball at his feet on a training pitch was something that fired him up.

Jez: I guess it's exactly that type of commitment and determination that has made him Spain's all-time top goal scorer, as well as the country's top World Cup scorer. Stay committed, keep the passion flowing, and you can achieve your goals.

CRISTIANO RONALDO

Billy: When Jez and I had the honour of appearing at the 2010 FIFA Ballon d'Or awards we were so nervous. We had the fear a bit. Performing in front of some of our idols and the world's greatest players can do that to a man.

Jez: This was the biggest performance of our lives to date and we had to wear suits all day for rehearsals. Then we were kept in a waiting room for nearly five hours – it was hot and uncomfortable. Imagine our nerves!

Billy: Adding to the stress was that we knew the stakes were so high. But we went out and absolutely smashed the routine – it was one of our best ever. As we got back to that sweaty waiting room, we were buzzing. A complete contrast to what we had felt like in there before. And the best was yet to come.

Jez: We'd only been sat there about 10 minutes when there was knock at the door. We opened it and it was none other than Cristiano Ronaldo standing

there. We couldn't believe our eyes! He congratulated us and told us the show was great.

Billy: Suddenly, that boiling hot room, the suits and all the nerves were all worthwhile. When someone at the top of the game tells you that you did an amazing job it's an indescribable feeling. We were buzzing!

PELÉ

Jez: When we're old grandfathers, sitting by the fireplace and looking back at all we achieved, I like to think we'll remember everything, however ropy our memories might get in old age. But one thing we will always remember, come what may, is the day we met Pelé.

Billy: What a privilege to meet and interview the greatest goal-scorer of all time.

Jez: Too right. The man scored 1,281 goals in 1,363 games, and if that's not tekkers then I don't know what is. But what we found was that, just as he was a total superstar of a player on the pitch, he couldn't be more humble off it.

Billy: Down to earth doesn't even begin to do justice to how modest this man is. Just to be in his presence was an honour. He watched videos of what

we do and said to us: 'This is not real, it is not possible.' It was unbelievable to hear those words from such a legend.

Jez: So for sure, we will never forget meeting him and learning from his experiences and words of wisdom. It's funny, when you look back at the video you can see we're a bit overwhelmed. We're a bit like nervous kids. But this was Pelé!

NEYMAR

Jez: When we filmed with this guy it was on a PES shoot over in Spain. Neymar had some media obligations before he could come over, meet up and do the filming. So, while Bill and I were setting up the pitches and cameras, we were told that Neymar would be over in about 10 minutes – and then were shown where he would be arriving from.

Bill: Jez is a clever lad, isn't he? He noticed that Neymar would be entering from the corner of the pitch so told me to leave a football where Neymar would be walking in. Just to see whether he would notice it and how he would react.

Jez: It was well worth setting that up. As he walked in he saw the ball and just whipped it from the corner into the goal – with zero bounce! We couldn't believe it – we thought maybe he might have started to do some kick-ups with it or perhaps pass the ball to me or Bill – but he went to a higher level.

Billy: He's got some serious tekkers. That was a good day!

F2 CHAPTER NINE

THE F2 STORY:
LIVING THE DREAM: THE F2

Jez: It's extremely demanding to perform in and run The F2. It doesn't just magically come together, you know! Don't get me wrong – I know we have the best jobs in the world. But we work tirelessly. It never ends. We work as many hours as we can in the day and night. Social media is 24/7. People naturally assume that we have a massive team behind us. I would assume that from outside, too. But it couldn't be further from the truth. Until very recently we did everything ourselves. Contracts, meetings, the talent on the day, editing, all the social networks – this is a full-time job! Recently, we've been signed by a fantastic management company called 10Ten Talent and it's great having them become part of our journey. Mark Upson helps us with the filming and editing.

Billy: Mark (right) tweeted us when he was 13 asking if he could interview us for his YouTube channel. I love people that are trying to make a name for themselves, so I said yes. He came and met us after one of our shoots at the London Soccer Dome and we did the interview.

Jez: You could see that he was a whiz kid with cameras. We stayed in touch and he often came and helped us on our shoots. When he left school we offered him a contract to come on board full-time. He's been an integral part of the team ever since and now we're looking to expand further.

Billy: It's just crazy, how big it has got. We have a set of very hardcore fans. They start up The F2 fan pages. They're from all over the world. They seem to know everything

'I KNOW WE HAVE THE BEST JOBS IN THE WORLD. BUT WE WORK TIRELESSLY.'

about our lives. We can 'like' a comment on Instagram and they will go and follow the people we've 'liked'. It's incredible that we've got that support.

Jez: And that's before we even get to the clothing range. Tell 'em about that, Bill.

Billy: It all started when we used to do live stage shows during the winter. It would be quite cold so we'd wear tracksuit bottoms. We needed to avoid the legs hanging over our feet so we decided to get them tailored ourselves. People started commenting: 'Where did you get those joggers from?' We decided we needed to own this and make a brand out of it. We were going to call it 'F2', but we wanted it to have an identity in its own right. We wanted footballers and celebrities to wear our range. We thought, would they wear our clothes if they were called 'F2'? Not sure! So we came up with the name 'Rascal'.

I flew to Turkey, having researched the best cotton manufacturers in the world. I was there for a week: I didn't leave until I had the best sample. A week later I placed the order. Then I had to look into trademarking the name, setting up the business properly and all the regulations you need for a clothing company.

Jez: It's like a pitch out of *Dragon's Den*. And, Bill, I'll give you all the money you're looking for, for 50 per cent of the company! Seriously, though, Billy has got such a talented business mind. He's a brilliant guy. He works so hard.

Billy: We invested quite a lot of money to get it going but we made that back on the very first day, so we knew that the F2 family loved the clothing. It's gone from strength to strength. Since then we've been getting out more ranges, adding more manpower. It was a lot of work but it had to be done.

RASCAL

We're so ambitious, me and Jez, that if we want to achieve something and we don't know how to do it, we'll research it and we won't stop until we know what we're doing. I think that's why we've been successful: if something's not working we'll find a way to make it work. That's just in our blood. Luckily for us, it has gone our way.

We started with Google. Researched the best clothing manufacturers. Went to clothes shops and looked inside the labels of the clothes, to find out what country they were made in. Asked questions on forums.

I arranged a ton of meetings and blagged it a bit where I needed to. I made out that I knew all about clothing and the industry, to make sure I wasn't ripped off. I kind of needed to do that. I went over with a suitcase full of samples and said: 'Replicate this with the best material you can.' One factory got it bang on, and we've been with them ever since.

It was scary but also fun to be in such a new world. Football has been part of my life since I was a kid. With the clothing I was stepping into the unknown. I've learned so much. We've been on par with Hype Clothing's first year. But they had a staff of 17 when I just had one customer services manager. So, even if I say so myself, we've done extremely well with Rascal.

We work so hard. I can't even tell you the last time I watched television. We just live and breathe The F2, as well as YouTube and Rascal. Alongside our families, that's our lives. We love it, we're addicted to it. We know we're living the best lives, we're living the dream.

Jez: Maybe we are living the dream... but it can tip over. Sometimes we go too far and work too hard.

Billy: Getting through winter is tough. Footballers' training involves cardio activity. Their heart rate goes up but they stay moving and warm. We're stop-start. We have periods of standing in the cold in shorts and T-shirts for 20 minutes or more. It may be raining or freezing. The hardest battle comes when we're feeling cold or we're wet and our muscles have cooled down and we have to produce the tekkers. It's the hardest thing to do.

I got ill once. I was in hospital for five days. I thought I was going to die! The doctors were taking it so seriously. I went to A&E. All night I'd been sweating and shivering. My wife, Katie, took me to the hospital. They did some tests and they said: 'Sir, you are really ill.' There were six doctors waiting for me and they rushed me in for an instant blood test.

My immune system was so low – through working so much and filming in freezing temperatures – I caught a virus. They didn't know what it was. It was something like dengue fever but I hadn't been anywhere tropical. Basically, I felt as if somebody was drilling through my bones. I was in agony. My temperature was extremely high; I was completely disorientated. Sick, fever. I had to have six injections and three blood tests a day. I had to be quarantined in hospital because they didn't know what it was.

I was there for four days but I was ill for more like nine days. My liver was in a terrible way. For a while it was really, really dangerous. It took a long time for me to recover. It was a bad time. I took a positive from the experience, though. Every morning now I wake up and I think back to that time when I was in hospital on a drip. My wife took a photo of me

looking very sick and I remind myself of how I was so that I can strive to be the best that I can; the fittest I can be. Any time I don't feel like going to the gym I remember how weak I was then. It drives me on, to be as far away from that as I can remember.

So I don't take it for granted any more that I can go onto a pitch and play. I had to take three weeks off when I was ill. I wasn't allowed to touch a football. I lost a stone. I'm a slight guy anyway. It was really, really tough. The whole thing was a massive wake-up call. I don't worry about silly little things. I might crack my phone screen or something, but in the grand scheme of things that doesn't matter. We're lucky.

Jez: It was hard to watch but it didn't come as a surprise, really. We had such

an intense winter, filming in the cold. Who else does what we do? Winter-sports people wear winter-sports appropriate clothing. We're standing around in the cold for hours in our shorts and T-shirts. We get absolutely freezing. I got ill that year, too. But he got ill worse.

Billy: It's all worth it, though. We have an amazing life and we never forget how lucky we are.

We've travelled the world and met some amazing people. Look at it all! The performance at the Ballon d'Or was an insane experience. We made history: the first freestylers to perform in front of the game's most important people.

So many other super cool things have happened. We met Pelé. I never thought that would be possible; to

'WE KNOW WE'RE LIVING THE BEST LIVES, WE'RE LIVING THE DREAM.'

share moments with him was incredible. I performed in the opening ceremony of the 2006 World Cup at Berlin's Brandenburg Gate for the fan fest. It was packed with about a million fans from all around the world.

We've filmed with some of the world's best footballers and they follow us! It's so weird to think that they're reading what we tweet. Makes you question what you tweet, I can tell you! A few of One Direction even follow us.

It's not just meeting big names that matters. We also love meeting our fans. I actually measure my success by how much people love what we do. When kids stop us to tell us what we mean to them, that's amazing. The other day we were walking into a hotel and I saw a kid recognise us. I waved at him and he froze. He started physically crying because he was so excited. That's a measure of success. He's crying because he met us. I see that and I feel successful because of the impact. I never thought we'd get to that level. It reminded me of me when I started to meet my heroes. When I first met Ronaldinho, I wasn't even in control of my body. I was so excited. To think that the kid I met in the hotel was so excited to meet me, when I'd been so excited to meet Ronaldinho. It makes me realise how cool the whole thing is.

Jez: And you know what a lot of this comes down to? We've thought of so many things in this game that nobody else has thought of. And we've actually done them! We think, wouldn't it be cool to… And then we go and do it. That's the first key difference between us and some other people.

GET THE SKILLS:
F2 AKKA

FACT FILE
ORIGIN: NEW EXCLUSIVE SKILL!
INVENTED BY JEREMY LYNCH, UK
SKILL TYPE: DRIBBLE
DIFFICULTY RATING: 10
TEKKERS RATING: 10
FREQUENTLY USED BY: MR J. LYNCH

Jez: I'm not going to lie to you, this skill should come with a warning: don't try this without a black belt in tekkers. It's tricky, but that's just the point. Bash this one out in a game and wait for the contract offers to start rolling in.

Roll the sole of your boot over the ball to flick it up, then bounce it off the outside of your calf, before immediately using your toe to knock it one way past a defender while you sprint as fast as you can round the other way.

Oh man, I love this one. I invented it exclusively for you in this book. That's right, you can't find out about this anywhere else. And neither can the defenders.

APPROACH THE DEFENDER

FLICK THE BALL UP

TOUCH THE BALL WITH THE OUTSIDE OF YOUR CALF

IMMEDIATELY FLICK OUT YOUR FOOT AND TOUCH THE BALL PAST YOUR OPPONENT

RUN ROUND THE OTHER SIDE OF THE DEFENDER

FLICK THE BALL UP...

TAP WITH THE OUTSIDE OF THE CALF...

BEFORE IT HITS THE GROUND, TOUCH IT FORWARDS

WASTE THE DEFENDER

TEKKERS MASTERS:
RONALDINHO

'HE WAS MY HERO, HE IS MY HERO, HE ALWAYS WILL BE. HE'S THE KING.'

RONALDINHO

SPEED: 8
VISION: 9
TOUCH: 10
FINISHING: 8
TEKKERS: 10

F2 TRUMPS

Billy: Meeting Ronaldinho was one of the most exciting moments of my life. He was just incredible. He was my hero, he is my hero, he always will be. He's the king.

He's got so much love to offer as a person. I started crying and he gave me a cuddle. I saw him three years later because I was going to perform at half-time and, when he saw me, he recognised me and gave me another hug. He remembered me! After I first met him I remember phoning everyone, jumping up and down, shaking. I was a proper fan!

Jez: Never known so much love. Ha, ha!

Billy: I can't help it, mate! The thing is, he's labelled the king for a reason. There is none greater than Ronaldinho. He always plays with a smile and total freedom. Just watching him is a treat. He's not a negative player; he never gets involved in violence or bad tackles. In

2006, when he was peaking, he revolutionised football. He did things no one had ever thought of doing or thought was possible.

Jez: The game is played at a faster and higher level right now, but before Messi, Neymar and Cristiano Ronaldo hit the scene, there was this guy – the Brazilian baller. He was a genius, full of mesmerising skills and tricks. I remember watching him and it was just infectious! A one-of-a-kind talent, which was proven by the trophies he won, and he won pretty much everything as a player. He played all over the attacking part of the action: as a central striker, out on the wing or, of course, as the classic number ten.

Billy: Some of that guy's skills defied the laws of physics, I swear. Let's go through his signature moves one by one. What about the elastico? A superb piece of skill that can totally fool your opponent – but you have to make sure you get it right! With your strong foot, you move the ball away from you – with the outside of the foot – then quickly pull it in with the inside.

Jez: Ronaldinho was good at it because he moved the ball away from his body so wide that everyone thought he was going that way. The elastico has been around for decades but he made it his own.

Billy: And the crazy thing is that the elastico was just one of so many tricks he could rock. His dribbling was insane and his overhead kicks were impossible, as were his feints in one-on-ones. And all

'HE WASN'T ONE TO STICK TO THE RULES WHEN THE RULES DIDN'T HELP HIM.'

those passes he did without even looking. Most coaches tell players all the time, 'Keep your eye on the ball!' But he wasn't one to stick to the rules when the rules didn't help him.

Jez: He wasn't one for caution – he's possibly the most uninhibited player I've seen in my lifetime. The hocus pocus is another fave. He'd pull the ball behind his leg with his outside foot, then whip it back around so it shifted direction instantly. Absolutely hypnotic stuff – and so crafty.

Billy: It felt like he invented a new skill every time he took to the field. But most of all I remember him gliding past defenders and his amazing close control of the ball. Imagine if he were as good at cards as he was at football? He'd rinse you – you'd never know what he was going to do next! He was a proper trickster, too. Will we ever see his like again?

Jez: Maybe Neymar has the best chance of living up to the standard he set. But it's a big ask. He won the lot. The World Cup in 2002 – we'll try and overlook that outrageous free kick that knocked out England – two La Ligas, the Champions League. The list goes on. Also all the big personal awards, including two Fifa World Player of the Year gongs and a cheeky Ballon d'Or.

Billy: And most importantly, he won hearts. Whoever you supported, you loved him. Even the Real Madrid fans gave him an ovation once. Barca beat them 3-0 at the Bernabeu and the Real fans actually gave him a standing ovation for his second goal on the night! He just swaggered past Ramos, pelted into the box and curled the ball past Casillas.

Recent European Championship winner Nani called him the 'best player in history'. That's a big shout. Well, I certainly can't think of any player who was better than him. He won us all over, all football fans. If you love football, you cannot help but love Ronaldinho. A wizard of a baller.

TOP 5 TEKKERS

WE'RE OFTEN ASKED QUESTIONS ABOUT THE PLAYERS WE'VE FILMED WITH. PEOPLE WANT TO KNOW WHO WAS THE BEST AT VARIOUS SKILLS AND WHICH PLAYER WAS THE FUNNIEST, WHO HAD THE BEST CLOBBER AND SO ON. SO HERE WE BREAK DOWN THE TOP 5 TEKKERS AND TELL YOU WHICH OF THE PLAYERS WE'VE MET RANKED HIGH ON EACH SCALE.

SKILL AND TRICKS
1. RONALDINHO
2. CRISTIANO RONALDO
3. NEYMAR
4. EDEN HAZARD
5. ZINEDINE ZIDANE

Why does Ronaldinho come top?

Billy: It's no secret that I'm a huge fan of this guy. He just had the complete package – he could do anything you wanted with a ball.

Jez: Erm, excuse me, Bill, I think you'll find a lot of us are huge fans of Ronaldinho. It's not just you! But anyway, if you're looking for an elite figure who almost bridged the worlds of professional football and freestyling, this is your man. He's been a mix of the two spheres from the start.

Billy: Ronaldinho was one of the most exciting modern-day footballers, and everyone liked to watch him play, thanks to his locker full of skills and tricks. I reckon what made him special is that he consistently did the unthinkable with the ball. He actually pulled off tricks that seemed to defy science.

Jez: Ha, you've gotta feel for anyone who played against him. As an opponent you'd pretty much just have to accept from the whistle that you're going to have a mare of an afternoon against this unpredictable wizard. He had to top this section.

Billy: He did. And I'd definitely top his fan club.

SHOT

1. STEVEN GERRARD
2. ZLATAN IBRAHIMOVIC
3. CRISTIANO RONALDO
4. GARETH BALE
5. DAVID VILLA

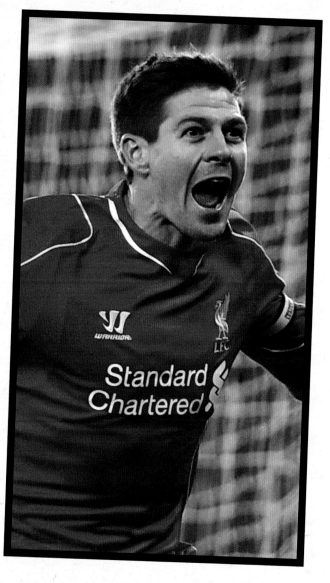

Why Gerrard?

Jez: Go inside your head and picture Steven Gerrard at his peak. OK, now come back. For most of you, I bet what just came to mind was an image of him driving home one of those masterful long shots he is so famous for.

Billy: That's what I just pictured – you absolute mind reader! When we filmed with Stevie G we got to see how amazing he is at sending those drives in. And it really is no fluke, he can do it time after time after time. It is actually unbelievable how he can generate so much power and accuracy in every shot. It makes for a winning combination.

Jez: He's scored some of the most memorable strikes in the last two decades. He's a Premier League legend. No matter what type of shot it was – whippage, volley, half-volley, knuckleball – they were all so consistently accurate. And whichever way you cut it, that is an amazing asset for a team to have.

Billy: That's it. You have all your strikers and wingers able to test out the opposition's back five, and then just when you think you've got them under control, you have this fella popping up from midfield too. What a baller. He just loves striking the ball.

TOUCH
1. LIONEL MESSI
2. MESUT ÖZIL
3. NEYMAR
4. RIYAD MAHREZ
5. JUAN MATA

Why Messi?

Billy: Once you've seen him up close and personal, you understand Messi at a new level. And when you get asked to film with Lionel Messi at the Barcelona training ground, that's not a decision it takes long to make.

Jez: Yeah, it's like: do we want to film with Messi at the Ciutat Esportiva Joan Gamper? Well, let me think… how about yes?

Billy: To be fair, we couldn't get over there quickly enough. Who wouldn't when they get an opportunity like that? And when we got there we got a whole new insight into what a great touch Messi has.

Jez: I mean, it's not like we didn't already know he has a sweet touch. Even if you don't like football you'll have heard that he's a bit nifty with the ball. Even your old gran knows that! Anyway, like we explained earlier, before we went on camera, Messi had to make a quick phone call on his mobile.

Billy: So while we were waiting for him to finish the call, Jez turns to me and says: 'Bill, ping a ball over to Messi and see what he does.' If I'd had time to think about it, I would have totally bottled that and not pinged it. But I did it.

Jez: So now let's look at this from Messi's point of view. He's casually having a chat on the phone when suddenly a pass he could never have expected races towards him. He had to react at literally the last moment. But he pulled it off with ease!

Billy: He did, he killed that ball dead. That's natural talent – being able to produce the goods at any moment, with zero notice. And that's why he's at the top of our touch league.

BANTER

1. **IAN WRIGHT**
2. **PIERRE-EMERICK AUBAMEYANG**
3. **MARCELO**
4. **DIEGO COSTA**
5. **MESUT ÖZIL**

Why Ian Wright?

Billy: Younger readers may only really know Wrighty from his television punditry, but you don't need to have watched him play to know that this guy is a pure bantersaurus.

Jez: When we were lucky enough to spend a whole day filming with this Arsenal legend we laughed from start to finish. He was just such a funny guy, always up for a laugh and a prank. If you spend time with Wrighty you just feel so much joy. He truly brings the best out in everyone he meets.

Billy: I've never met anyone with a bigger heart and love for life than him. He just loves to be alive, and he loves football in particular, doesn't he? He's like a big kid in the best of ways. He hasn't lost that innocent love of football that we all have as children.

Jez: He's also really nice. Despite being so famous and popular he's totally down to earth – a proper man of the people. Guys who played with him at Arsenal can't speak highly enough of him. They say he was just such a funny and kind man. Having met him we can only agree.

Billy: Even now, when I think back to that day, I can hear that cheeky laugh of his in my head. What a brilliant character.

SWAG

1. PAUL POGBA
2. ANDREA PIRLO
3. NEYMAR
4. PIERRE-EMERICK AUBAMEYANG
5. MESUT ÖZIL

Why Pogba?

Jez: There were some strong contenders for this list but it was the man Pogba who just edged it to finish on top. He's not just football's most expensive player, he's football's top swag man. The way he brings music, fashion and football together, with such nonchalance, is very special.

Billy: So let's take it from the top. Pogba's hair is always on point. His clothes game is strong, too. In short, he always looks fresh and sharp. You never see him walking down the road looking shabby. There's no day off when you're Paul Pogba.

Jez: He just oozes coolness, right? Look at his handshake tekkers with team mates. Him and guys like Eric Bailly have got all the hand moves down to a fine art. Pogba's even cool on social media – check out his bromance with Zlatan.

Billy: We're loving his dancing, too. His goal celebrations light up the game as much as the strikes themselves. He always hits the Dab, on and off the pitch. The whole thing just oozes coolness and adds up to the ultimate swag package, 24/7. He's nearly as cool as me!

Jez: I have no words…

CHAPTER
TEN

THE F2 STORY:
STYLING IT OUT: THE F2

Billy: We've learned so much about how to make it work on YouTube. We feel blessed. It would be nice to share what we've learned.

Jez: Agreed. You know, you can pick up a lot yourself just by looking carefully. Success leaves clues. I would recommend you study the top YouTubers and social influencers and try and look for things that they've done well. I think having a niche is tremendously important.

It's about dedication and hard work. They stay up late and they wake up early. Be prepared for it to take over your life. Every hour we film means three or four hours editing for me. At least. In a normal week I'll spend 16–25 hours editing. It pays off!

Personality is important. Let your personality shine, so people can relate to you and feel like they know you. That's the difference between a YouTuber and a conventional TV personality. Viewers must feel that they know you, that there's no barrier.

Billy: With freestyling videos, it's so important to make it appear effortless. It's just part of being cool, isn't it? It's so cool to do something really hard and make it look easy. Tiger Woods did that in golf. You know when you do, say, crossbar challenge, you know as soon as you've hit it if it's worked. It's like instinct.

This whole thing of pulling off amazing tricks and playing it cool, the kids have really embraced it. They'll send us videos of them slamming the ball into the top corner and then walking away really cool. It feels so great that we created this.

Remember that famous Eric Cantona goal for Man Utd when he did a dink and then just stood there as the ground went crazy? I don't know how people in actual football games manage that. When I play in games I have to run away and celebrate. So I look at people like Balotelli when they score and then they don't move. The composure! I don't know how they pull it off on the football field.

'VIEWERS MUST FEEL THAT THEY KNOW YOU, THAT THERE'S NO BARRIER.'

The key to freestyle and YouTube is to think outside the box. Make your content original and people want to see it. We both feel that football freestyle is something like 80 per cent practice. The remaining 20 per cent is where the originality kicks in. That imaginative spark that makes it special.

Humour is important, too, in my opinion. People watch our YouTube videos for two reasons: to learn and to be entertained. It's these two vital ingredients that make The F2 videos what they are.

But nothing can replace dedication. We practise our freestyling moves so hard. We have to really put time and patience into it by practising it over again and over again.

Jez: And over and over again.

Billy: And over again…

Jez: … and over again. We originally saw YouTube as a route to mainstream television. But over time we've found that it stands on its own as our focus. That said, we enjoyed our dips into television and we'd like to do more.

Billy: We got approached by a company who wanted to do a TV show for the London Live channel in 2015. It was called *F2 Kicks Off*. We went around completing public challenges. Each episode we had to amaze the public. Music artists like Lethal Bizzle, Wretch 32 and Tinchy Stryder as

'BETWEEN US WE'VE GOT EIGHT GUINNESS WORLD RECORDS.'

well as other celebrities would give us the challenges.

Jez: London Live was amazing. The company called us: 'We want to pitch you for a TV show. Do you mind?'

We said: 'Of course, crack on. If something comes of it, good. If it doesn't then nothing lost.' I didn't expect them to come back with a show commissioned before they'd even met us in person!

It was class, man. Exploring the city. Loved it. It was the most successful commission on the whole network by a landslide. We were very proud of that. We were pushing towards 300,000 viewers and their next biggest show was below 100,000.

Billy: We also got a segment on *Soccer AM*, Sky Sports' Saturday morning show. A huge TV institution, that. We'd grown up watching it. We got told it was one of the most successful parts of the show they'd ever had.

Jez: *Soccer AM* was a big thing for us because we were fans of the show from when we were kids. To get the opportunity was a big deal. People still come up to us about that, too. Our segment went down really, really well. It comes back to our policy – everything with excellence.

Between us we've got eight Guinness World Records. We've got individual ones and joint ones as The F2. I had 'longest distance travelling with the ball on the head'. Bill had 'longest distance travelled catching the ball on

the neck and flicking it back up'. We have to get an official out to watch us and we find out right away whether or not we've done it. I've got all the certificates at home. Framed. Really good. In 2011, I was labelled as the *Soccer AM* ultimate Skill Skool champion.

Billy: These are like our equivalents of the medals that mainstream footballers get.

Jez: But I do believe it wasn't our destiny or our fate to be playing in the Prem or in any top league as pros. What we were meant to do is what we're doing now – The F2. It's very clear now but at the time it was hard. When Arsenal let me go I was distraught. I couldn't see why this was happening. I didn't understand it. And then we became mates by going into tricks. We crossed paths, got on well, and ended up a double act. Both on the same wavelength, both get along really well. Both got creative minds, both get it, both understand social media. We're also both attuned to what people are entertained by, what they want to see.

We live within 30 minutes of each other so we could meet up easily from the start. We both were willing to commit. All up, it's amazing. We're a similar age, similar height and build. There's a lot of parameters that have come together. It works… it works… it works. We've even got complementary personalities. It was definitely meant to be and I believe it's proper fate.

We both really respect each other's views on everything. We've reached a point where if one of us feels really strongly about something, the other will go with it whatever the feeling on the other side. It's a good way to be, it rewards passion. Let people express their passions.

Billy: Jez is very headstrong and determined, lots of drive. I'm into the business side; he's more creative. I'll be thinking about how we can progress as a brand and he will be coming out with routines and concepts.

The north London rivalry doesn't affect us at all. I go to Spurs games, pay for tickets and I love it. But Arsenal do always seem to outdo Spurs and he will wind me up sometimes, though. Just little subtle digs.

We look at a much bigger picture. We're determined people. We're winners. We don't like losing or failing. We're not settlers, we want the best of the best.

Jez: The Arsenal/Spurs thing doesn't have a huge impact on us. We don't get that much into it with each other. We have to work together so if we were constantly digging each other out about our teams that wouldn't work. There's only so long you can talk about derby rivalries. It could get silly. Why would we focus on the one thing that divides us?

In the future we want to go so much more epic. I've got future chapters and plans already in my head. We're not naïve; we know anything can happen in life. We've made sure we have other options as fall-backs. I'm a qualified Uefa B coach, so I can coach up to academy level at any club. That was part of my sports degree. Actually, I should say that I did an IQ test last year and got a 161. It was a problem-solving IQ test and it's a decent score. Billy is the most switched on guy I know. That combination of him and me has definitely helped in our journey to become a leading football social media force.

Billy: All right, Jez…

Jez: At the moment, everything is unbelievable, so it's all about maintaining what we have. We are becoming footballing social-media powerhouses and massive global influencers. If we think the numbers we have are frightening now, then imagine them in a few years. We're aiming high. With that, comes opportunity, power and a whole lot of responsibility. This is our passion. So we will be building something we love.

It's important for us to inspire young people to reach their goals, whatever that target is. Whether it's within freestyling, the wider game or whatever else a young person wants to achieve.

I genuinely believe that Bill and me are living proof that if you put your mind to something then, no matter what your circumstances, you can reach your dream with practice, determination and sheer willpower.

We want to reach 100 million. As I speak here, we have 10 million followers. So it's a big target. We believe we can do it. Don't bet against us. We also want to set a good example to kids. We want to make our fans happy and show them how to be epic. Because none of this could have been possible without you. So thank you so much for coming on this incredible journey with us.

Billy: Absolutely. There are bigger and better things to come and we want you all to be involved. Thank you for being a part of the F2 family – we couldn't have done it without you.

So that's the end of our story… for now. Bring on the next chapter, and until then – love, peace and tekkers.

GET THE SKILLS:
WHIPPAGE

FACT FILE

ORIGIN: UNKNOWN
SKILL TYPE: SHOT
DIFFICULTY RATING: 8
TEKKERS RATING: 9
FREQUENTLY USED BY: LIONEL MESSI,
DAVID BECKHAM, ANDREA PIRLO

Jez: This is Whippage. Lionel Messi-style. Watch how the Argentinian master takes his free kicks. The amount of bend he puts on the ball is just unreal. Top corner every time. But how does he do it?

The trick is to start your run-up side-on. Make sure you strike the ball with your in-step, and then, as you follow through, land on the same foot that you struck the ball with. That's what gets that extra swaz.

The more you practice this one, the easier it gets. And, when your team gets that free-kick in the last minute of the game, guess who's going to be ready to step up…

APPROACH THE BALL SIDE ON

STRIKE THE BALL WITH YOUR INSTEP

FOLLOW THROUGH SO THAT THE FOOT
THAT STRUCK THE BALL LANDS FIRST

SIDE-ON

INSTEP

FOLLOW THROUGH

THIS IS...

...WHIPPAGE

TEKKERS MASTERS:
PELÉ

'HIS BOX OF TRICKS WAS SO FULL IT WAS EXPLODING!'

PELÉ

SPEED: 9
VISION: 8
TOUCH: 8
FINISHING: 10
TEKKERS: 7

F2 TRUMPS

Jez: Time for a bit of old-school tekkers now. You can't get much better than Pelé, can you? He defined football over three decades: the 1950s, the '60s and the '70s. His goal record speaks for itself.

Billy: Definitely. He's the daddy of all football history. If you want to talk about pure class in the game then you really have to measure it against him. You keep coming back to him over and over again. And he didn't just have the class, he won the silverware to back it up.

Jez: Three world cups? Three?! This one man grabbed two more world cups than England! He played in 1,367 matches and scored 1,283 goals. He scored eight goals in one game alone. How do you get that good?

Billy: Mate, he didn't even have a football as a kid in Brazil. Where he grew up, people didn't have much, so he got a sock and rammed it full of old rags and kicked that about to learn his trade. By 15 he was already a professional in Santos, São Paulo and by 17 he was a world champion. How outrageous is that?

Jez: So what do we think made the man so special?

Billy: His box of tricks was so full it was exploding! I like his runaround trick. When a team-mate passed him the ball, he would sell his opponent the best dummy you can imagine – he'd pretend to go for the ball but let it run past them both, then he'd whip around the opponent and pick up the play.

'PREPARE, RESPECT YOUR OPPONENT AND NEVER THINK YOU ARE THE BEST.'

Jez: Ha, ha! See ya later!

Billy: When you haven't got much time and space, that move will unlock the game. But it's harder than it sounds. You've got to be a class apart to pull it off.

Jez: And Pelé is an absolute class apart. Mate, how nervous were we when we met him? I felt like I was meeting a head teacher or something!

Billy: There we were telling him how we make our videos and he says he'll go in one!

Jez: We'll never forget the day we met him, will we? And his words that day should be heard by anyone who wants to make it as a pro: 'Prepare, respect your opponent and never think you are the best.'

Billy: Sound advice – although, in his case, he is the best! Come on, he's got to be

up there. He watched our videos, turned around to us and said: 'This is not real.' It's got to be the biggest compliment of all time, hasn't it? When Pelé says your football talent is not real. I mean, when did it get to that stage?

Jez: Let's say it out loud again: we've met Pelé.

Billy: We've actually met Pelé!

Jez: And he liked us! Pelé liked us! If anything makes all our hard work and dedication worthwhile, it's that. He's a legend. Did you know that the Corinthians' goalkeeper who was between the sticks when Pelé slotted home his first-ever goal whacked that fact on his business cards? He had emblazoned across them that he was the goalkeeper who let in Pelé's first goal.

Billy: Ha! What a lad!

FRIENDS OF THE F2

@_ITSJJ
@19TMB
@22DEMARAI
@433
@ADAMWAITHE
@ADAMWOODYAT
@ADIDASUK
@ADLENEGUEDIOURA
@ALIA
@ANESONGIB
@AUBAMEYANG7
@BARCLAYBEALES
@BATESON87
@BEHZINGA
@BIG_BLACKS
@BLINDDALEY
@BRAD_SMITH94
@BRODIESMITH21
@CALFREEZY
@CALLUX
@CALUMBEST
@CAPGUNTOM
@CASTRO1021
@CHARLIEJONES
@CHARLIESLOTH
@CHRISGUNTER16
@CHRISMD10
@COMEDYGAMER
@CONNORNIGEL
@CRAIGDAVID
@DALLAGLIO8
@DANNYCIPRIANI
@DANNYO
@DAVIDVILLA
@DELE_ALLI
@DJTARGET
@DOMSOLANKE
@DREAMTEAMFC

@DUDEPERFECT
@DWIGHTGAYLE
@EDERLOPESOFICIAL
@FANTASYHACHI
@FREEKICKERZ
@FRIMPONGED10
@FUCHS_OFFICIAL
@FUCHSOFFICIAL
@GLENNHODDLE
@GONTH93
@GUAJE7VILLA
@GYASINHO
@HARRYWINKS
@HAZARDEDEN_10
@HDGOMES
@HUGHWIZZY
@IAM_OBJXIII
@IANWRIGHT0
@INDICOWIE
@ITSJAKEMITCHELL
@JACK_MAYNARD23
@JACKJONESTV
@JAKEBOYS
@JAKEJMITCHELL
@JAKESIMS
@JAMALEDWARDS
@JAMIEOLIVER
@JASPERCILLESSEN
@JAYRODRIGUEZ_9
@JBUTLAND_
@JENNA_MARBLES
@JIMMYBULLARD
@JIMMYCONRAD
@JJENAS8
@JMXFIFA
@JOE_WELLER_
@JUANMATA8
@KICK
@KOKE6
@KSCHMEICHEL1

@KSI
@LEETRUNDLE10
@LEWIS_NEAL24
@LEWISBLOOR1
@LOUIS_TOMLINSON
@LOUIST91
@LUKASZFABIANSKI
@M10_OFFICIAL
@MANNY_OFFICIAL
@MARCUSBUTLER
@MATTHDGAMER
@MELISSAJOANHART
@MENINBLAZERS
@MICHAILANTONIO
@MINIMINTER
@MRDAVIDHAYE
@MRGEORGEBENSON
@NC22BACK
@NCHADLI
@NEPENTHEZ
@NEWHOPEREECE
@NEWYORKREDBULLS
@NIALLOFFICIAL
@NYCFC
@OAKELFISH
@OBJ_3
@OFFICIALMGH
@OFFICIALWRETCH32
@OMGITSALIA
@PHILLJONES4
@PRODIRECTSOCCER
@REALAKINFENWA
@REALDENISEWELCH
@REECEOXFORD_
@RICKYRAYMENT
@ROBBIEKEANE
@ROS5IHD
@ROSSBARKLEY
@RUDIMENTALUK
@SAMBAILEYREAL
@SAMKINGFTW

@SAMPEPPER
@SCHMELLE_29
@SEANFREESTYLE
@SEUNGWOOLEE
@SKILLTWINS
@SKYSPORTSALEXH
@SMITHYSOCCERAM
@SOCCERAM
@SPENFC
@STARTERBLKLABEL
@STEVENCAULKER4
@STEVENGERRARD
@SWP29
@SYLVIANDISTIN
@THEHUNNABAND
@THELEANMACHINE-
SOFFICIAL
@THEOFFICIALAC3
@THEOWALCOTT
@THEREALBWP
@THEREEVHD
@TIMHOW1
@TOBJIZZLE
@TOMKINSOFFICIAL
@TOUZANITV
@TSBIBLE
@TUBESSOCCERAM
@TWOSYNCOFFICIAL
@TYBRACEY
@WES5L1NK
@WHISTLESPORTS
@WILFRIEDZAHA
@WILLIANBORGES88
@WRETCH32
@WRIGHTYOFFICIAL
@WROETOSHAW
@YANNICKBOLASIE
@YIANNIMIZE
@YOUTUBE
@ZERKAAHD

TEKKERS
PRACTICE JOURNAL

The best pros plan their practice to eliminate their weaknesses. Keep track of your journey to becoming a superstar here.

Shade in the diagram to show hours practiced

SKILL	BEGINNER 2hrs			AMATEUR 4hrs			EXPERT 6hrs		
NO-LOOK PASS									
ELECTRIC TWIST									
LYNCH FLIP-FLAP									
NEYMAR TOUCH TEKKERS									
RABONA									
WINGROVE CRUYFF									

PRO	SUPERSTAR	ATTACH PHOTO
8hrs	10hrs	

TEKKERS
PRACTICE JOURNAL

The best pros plan their practice to eliminate their weaknesses. Keep track of your journey to becoming a superstar here.

Shade in the diagram to show hours practiced

SKILL	BEGINNER 2hrs	AMATEUR 4hrs	EXPERT 6hrs
RONALDO KNUCKLEBALL			
BACK SNAP			
F2 AKKA			
WHIPPAGE			
YOUR OWN SKILL			
YOUR OWN SKILL			

PRO 8hrs	SUPERSTAR 10hrs	ATTACH PHOTO

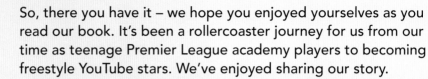

So, there you have it – we hope you enjoyed yourselves as you read our book. It's been a rollercoaster journey for us from our time as teenage Premier League academy players to becoming freestyle YouTube stars. We've enjoyed sharing our story.

We're now deep into 'time added on' in our book, so we'd like to leave you with one final message – and it's a crucial one, guys. If you want to make it as a freestyler, a footballer, or in pretty much any sport, practice is important.

So practise, practise and then practise some more. Stay humble and enjoy yourselves.

Love, peace and tekkers, The F2.

ACKNOWLEDGEMENTS

Billy: Thank you to all my family who have always been there for me. My family means everything to me: Kate, who has supported me through it all from the very start of my career, Amelie with the super dancing skills, who thinks her dad is better than Lionel Messi, and baby Roman who is already showing off some great football tekkers.

Finally I would like to thank all of the Wingrove family. As you can see from the photo on the left, there are too many to name them all, but through the ups and downs they have been there supporting me every step of the way and I couldn't ask for a better family.

Thank you and I love you all x

Jez: I want to take this opportunity to thank my family, who have offered me guidance on every step of this incredible journey. Dad, for the countless hours you spent at the park with me as a kid; Mum, for your constant love and support; and to both of you for always believing in me through the highs and the lows.

Thanks to my brother Christopher for being my best friend; and to my two sisters, Charlotte and Cara, for putting up with their older brother for all these years.

Thank you for always being there for me x

Billy and Jez: We'd also like to say a massive thank you to our amazing team at 10Ten Talent – especially Terry Byrne, Louie Evans, Tom Caplan and Luke Aldridge. They are a major part of The F2 Family and we love having them with us on our incredible and super exciting journey.

A big thank you must go to the guys at Blink Publishing, including our editors Joel Simons and Matt Phillips; designers Steve Leard and Nathan Balsom; Chas Newkey-Burden and Joanna de Vries; not forgetting Ben Dunn, Lisa Hoare, Karen Browning, Beth Eynon and Michelle Tilley. This book is something we are so proud of and they have all been brilliant to work with. Finally, thanks to Jonathan Marks and his crew at MTC for connecting the dream team.

Big love, too, to all the amazing brands and teams within the agencies who have chosen to work with The F2. Without them, we wouldn't be able to create such cool and innovative videos that break boundaries and continue to excite you guys. We love being Adidas ambassadors and a big shout out to Ben Goldhagen and his team, who have been so passionate about us from the beginning.

Finally, we are so grateful to all the players who have been part of so many incredible videos. They challenge us to be better every day, and we really appreciate their time and commitment to make such great content for The F2 Family.

WE ARE THE F2

...and this is our *World of Football.* Inside we give away the biggest secrets of the greatest footballers on the planet. Want tricks like **Neymar**? Or to hit free-kicks like **Ronaldo**? Or to dribble like **Messi**? We show you how.

We've been travelling the world, meeting the biggest stars, like **Gareth Bale, Ronaldinho, Mesut Özil, Pelé** and **Stevie G**, and now we give you the lowdown on what they're really like, and how they got their edge.

We'll also let you in on our journey from aspiring pros to **YouTube superstars** with over **10 million** followers. Want to know how to become a social media star? **That's inside too!**

There's a **free app** to download that will make the pages come to life with exclusive videos, tricks and games. **So, what are you waiting for?** Open, read, learn, download and get out on the pitch and practise.

Love, peace and tekkers,

BILLY & JEZ AKA THE F2

ISBN 978-1-91127-476-6

BLINK
bringing you closer

UK £14.99

www.blinkpublishing.co.uk

Photography © Dan Rouse
Cover Design by Nathan Balsom

KU-394-114